How

Getting into Canada

Books to change your life and work.
Accessible, easy to read and easy to act on –
other titles in the **How To** series include:

Living & Working in Canada
A new life in Canada – all you need to know

Getting a Job in Canada
Secure a well-paid job and a great new lifestyle

Getting a Job Abroad
The handbook for the international jobseeker: where the jobs are, how to get them

Spending a Year Abroad
A guide to opportunities for self-development and discovery around the world

Finding Voluntary Work Abroad
All the information you need for getting valuable work experience overseas

The **How To** series now contains
around 200 titles in the following categories:

Business & Management
Career Choices
Career Development
Computers & the Net
Creative Writing
Home & Family
Living & Working Abroad
Personal Development
Personal Finance
Self-Employment & Small Business
Study Skills & Student Guides

For full details, please send for a free copy
of the latest catalogue to:

How To Books
3 Newtec Place, Magdalen Road
Oxford OX4 1RE, United Kingdom
e-mail: info@howtobooks.co.uk
http://www.howtobooks.co.uk

Getting into Canada

How to make a successful application for permanent residence

M. J. BJARNASON
2nd edition

How To Books

Published by How To Books Ltd,
3 Newtec Place, Magdalen Road,
Oxford OX4 1RE, United Kingdom.
Tel: (01865) 793806. Fax: (01865) 248780.
email: info@howtobooks.co.uk
http://www.howtobooks.co.uk

First edition 1996
Second edition 2001

British Library Cataloguing in Publication Data.
A catalogue record for this book is available from
the British Library.

Cartoons by Mike Flanagan
Cover design by Shireen Nathoo Design
Cover image by PhotoDisc

Produced for How To Books by Deer Park Productions
Typeset by Kestrel Data, Exeter
Printed and bound by Cromwell Press Ltd, Trowbridge, Wiltshire

Contents

List of Illustrations

Preface

The Canadian immigration process is difficult to understand for applicants who, as a result, are disadvantaged in submitting their applications. In addition, applicants often are unable to obtain straightforward information from Canadian Immigration authorities.

In fact, at the present time, at least, applicants can expect delay, no communication, no response to inquiries and an overall mentality which seems to frustrate and obstruct and delay their application. Although this is not the intention of the Immigration Department, it is a matter of fact.

This book is intended to demystify the process by providing prospective immigrants with the information necessary to assess their qualifications beforehand. They can submit their applications with a complete knowledge of the procedures and enhance their prospects of success.

Based on more than 35 years' experience, *Getting Into Canada* has been written to aid prospective immigrants to Canada, primarily persons residing outside Canada who wish to follow the legal process to become permanent residents of Canada. It tells how to complete, document and submit an application with confidence.

It applies to all provinces and territories of Canada except for the Province of Quebec which has its own immigrant selection system. The Quebec selection system is very complex and of course usually requires some knowledge of the French language. If you wish to settle in Quebec, you will need to contact a consultant or lawyer who specialises in the Quebec Immigration selection process.

Getting Into Canada includes the necessary sample forms, addresses, charts, information and recommendations needed to assess your own qualifications and properly submit your application.

My objective is to help you to maximise your chances of success.

This book is designed to offer you a clear understanding of Canadian immigration procedures, so that you may determine whether or not you can comply with the requirements. It explains how to go about applying for permanent residence, and what to expect as you go through each stage of the procedure.

Getting Into Canada is presented in simple language, without any direct reference to sections of the Immigration Act and Regulations. I want you to be able to use it as a practical and step-by-step guide to the Canadian immigration process. The book outlines the different categories in which you can apply and helps you determine which is best suited to your circumstances.

You are then guided through the process that you will have to follow, from the gathering of information and documentation for the application to actually coming to Canada as an immigrant. In short, this book should answer all the essential questions you have if you are contemplating emigrating to Canada.

AN IMPORTANT NOTE

On 6 April 2000 the Minister of Citizenship and Immigration introduced a new Immigration Act to the Canadian House of Commons. This was reviewed by the Standing Committee on Citizenship and Immigration. Unfortunately the new Immigration Act died on the Order Paper because of the election in December 2000. It will most likely be re-introduced early in 2001. Nevertheless, here are the most important 'probable' changes that will affect the processing of the future applications of immigrants to Canada:

- Applicants will be dealt with more quickly (we hope).

- The definition of a 'dependent child' will increase from under 19 to under 22 years of age.

- Adoption provisions will be opened up in keeping with the best interest of the child.

- The definition of family class will be modernised in accordance with government legislation – the family class will include spouses, common-law and the same sex partners.

- An 'in-Canada' landing class will be created for sponsored spouses and partners.

- Sponsored spouses and dependent children will be exempted from the admission bar related to excessive demand on health or social services.

- The age at which Canadian Citizens or Permanent Residents are eligible to sponsor will be reduced from 19 to 18 years of age.

- The selection system for skilled workers will be modernised: this means moving away from the present occupation-based model to one focused on flexible and transferable skills. It also means assigning more weight to education and having a knowledge of English or French.

- The Temporary Worker Programme will be expanded: this means creating an in-land landing class for temporary workers, including students within Canada who have been working legally in Canada, to land within Canada.

- Business Immigration: it is very unclear what the government has in mind for entrepreneurs and investors, but it seems a new definite net financial requirement for entrepreneurs will be required, and probably applicants employing at least five people will be eligible.

- Permanent Residence: it is proposed to introduce a clear requirement that to retain permanent status, a person would have to be physically in Canada for a cumulative period of 2 years in every 5 working years.

Please keep in mind that the above are only some of the main proposals to the Immigration Act that would primarily affect applicants who wish to apply in the proper manner.

If these amendments come into effect, probably more through Regulations under the new Immigration Act, rather than as part of the Act itself, you may find yourself in a much better position to file an application successfully, as it is clear that Immigration is opening its door wider.

However, what you read in this book **refers to the present legislation and requirements**.

M. J. Bjarnason

1

The Immigration Categories

In order to begin the process of assessing your prospects of successfully immigrating, it is necessary that you have a knowledge of the basic immigration categories and some specific definitions. I will explain these as simply as possible.

Basically, there are only two categories under which you can apply to become a permanent resident of Canada: **Sponsored Dependant** and **Independent Applicant**.

The following definitions will make it easier for you to understand the two main categories and the various subsections under the independent category.

SPONSORED DEPENDANTS

These are close relatives of a Canadian citizen or of a permanent resident who is at least 19 years of age. Relatives eligible for admission in this category include:

- husband or wife

- fiancé or fiancée with accompanying dependent children

- father or mother

- dependent children

- grandparents

- unmarried orphaned brothers, sisters, nephews, nieces or grandchildren under 19 years of age.

There are certain very limited exceptions under which you can apply as a Sponsored Dependant even if you are not very closely related to a Canadian citizen or permanent resident.

For example, if you have a relative of any degree who is a Canadian citizen or permanent resident who has no very close relatives in Canada or anywhere else in the world, you might be able to be sponsored by that person as a Sponsored Dependant. Your relative in Canada would have to be unmarried (or divorced) and without children, parents or grandparents. It should be noted that this exception rarely applies, as most people have a close relative somewhere.

If you think you might fall into this category, or there are other very special circumstances about your situation, it would be best for you or your relative in Canada to seek the advice of a professional immigration consultant.

INDEPENDENT APPLICANTS

There are four categories of Independent Applicants:

- Skilled Immigrants
- Entrepreneurs
- Investors
- Self-Employed

Skilled Immigrants

Skilled Immigrants are individuals intending to seek employment in Canada in an occupation which is in demand. (An arranged job in Canada is *not* necessary, although it helps.)

Entrepreneurs

Entrepreneurs are persons who have the intention and ability to establish, purchase, or make a substantial investment in a business venture in Canada in which *the applicant will actively be involved in the management of the business.*

The business must make a significant contribution to the economy and result in the creation or maintenance of employment opportunities for at least one or more Canadian citizens or permanent residents, other than the entrepreneur and his dependants. This category is attractive to experienced business persons whose background is oriented towards the ownership and management of small to medium-sized enterprises.

Investors

Investors are persons who have a proven managerial track record in business, and have a personal net worth of Can$800,000 or more. Investors are required to make an investment of a minimum of Can$400,000 for at least five (5) years in a specific project or investment syndicate. Since 1 July 1996, applicants are only allowed to invest in government-administered venture capital funds. The only exception is in the Province of Quebec where investments can be made in privately administered investment syndicates.

Self-Employed

A Self-Employed immigrant is a person who has the intention and ability to establish a business in Canada that will employ only the applicant. The business must make a significant contribution to the economy, or to the cultural or artistic life of Canada. This category accommodates individuals who, although they may not create or preserve jobs for Canadians, nevertheless make a significant contribution in economic and artistic terms, such as farmers, sports personalities, artists, authors, members of the performing arts, and operators of small outlets which certain communities may need.

WITHDRAWN CATEGORIES

Retirement Category

It was previously possible to apply as a Retired Person. This provision of the Immigration Regulations has been withdrawn. It is no longer possible for an applicant without relatives in the Sponsored Dependant category in Canada to apply on the basis of retirement.

Assisted Relatives

Prior to February 1993, it was possible for a Canadian citizen or permanent resident to sponsor a brother, sister, uncle, aunt, nephew or niece for admission into Canada. This provision of the Immigration Regulations has been rescinded. Such relatives must now comply as Independent Applicants, although they will receive some limited benefit for having a relative in Canada. As noted in the Preface, impending changes in the Regulations may make it possible to sponsor a close relative (without regard to occupational requirements).

ACCOMPANYING FAMILY MEMBERS

New Immigration Regulations have been implemented which determine who may be included in the Canadian immigration application of the principal applicant and his/her spouse for the purpose of accompanying them to live in Canada. Formerly, all never married children of any age could be included as dependants on their parents' application, regardless of whether they were in fact truly dependent on their parents.

New definition

The present regulations allow you to include on your application as your accompanying dependants only the following:

(1) Your and/or your spouse's unmarried children under age 19 at the time your application is submitted. They must be unmarried when they apply for a visa, and still unmarried when the visa is issued.

(2) A son or daughter who is 19 or over at the time the application is submitted, but who is continuously enrolled and in attendance as a full-time student in an academic, professional or vocational programme at a university, college or other educational institution, and has been during that time wholly or substantially financially supported by his/her parents. Such a child could be married.

(3) A son or daughter of any age who is suffering from a physical or mental disability, is wholly or substantially supported by his/her parents and is incapable of supporting him/herself by reason of that disability.

(4) The unmarried children under age 19 of the persons referred to in (1) to (3) above.

Key points concerning children

There are some important points to remember when deciding which children can be included as accompanying dependants on your application form:

• Your dependants, to be eligible to accompany you to Canada, must be able to show that they meet the foregoing requirements regarding marital status and dependency both at the time the application for permanent residence is received by the immigration office and when the immigrant visa is ready to be issued. For example, if a child over 19 is a full-time student when an application is submitted, but has left school by the time the case is finalised, he/she will no longer be eligible to be included on your application.

- A child under 19 when the application is submitted but over 19 when it is ready to be finalised is *not* disqualified as a result of passing the age limit while the application is in process.

- If you have a child over 19 whom you believe meets the requirements set out in paragraphs (2) or (3) above and is thereby eligible to be included in your application, you must:

  (a) clearly indicate this fact on your application and provide information and documentation in respect of that child with your application, such as letters of acceptance from your dependants' educational institutions, cancelled cheques showing tuition, room or board you have paid or other papers telling how you support your dependants,

  (b) attach a written explanation to your application form indicating why this child is dependent upon you, and

  (c) submit any required processing fees in respect of that child, pursuant to the instructions regarding fee payment which are included in the application package.

Finally, it should be noted that your ineligible children are not by their exclusion from your application disqualified from later immigrating to Canada. However, they must at the time when they wish to proceed meet the selection criteria in the appropriate immigration category.

HOW TO CHOOSE THE RIGHT CATEGORIES

Let us consider how best to opt for the right category. First, go back to the definition of the Sponsored Dependant category.

Do you have any of those relatives in Canada who are at least 19 years of age and willing and able to help you?

If you do, you are in the best possible position to have an application approved.

If you do not have a relative in the Sponsored Dependant category, do you or your spouse have a relative (closer than a cousin) who is a Canadian citizen or permanent resident, 19 years of age or over, and willing to help you?

If you do, that's good. It's not as good as having a relative under the Sponsored Dependant category in Canada, but it does put you in a better position to be successful in your application to emigrate.

Do you have substantial assets and business experience?

If so, you may be able to submit an application as an Entrepreneur, Self-Employed person or Investor.

If you do not have a relative in Canada and your assets are limited, you should not abandon hope of immigrating to Canada.

Remember, you may also apply to come to Canada to take up employment as a skilled immigrant. There might be very few people in Canada with your qualifications, and your occupation might be strongly in demand. If so, your application may be accepted under the General Occupations List which are detailed in Chapter 3.

Don't be concerned if you have not fully understood these various options. As we proceed, each will be dealt with in turn as we go through the application process.

A CAUTIONARY NOTE

Before we begin to describe the application process, there is one piece of advice applicable to every case.

> **Do not write or say anything throughout the application process that is not truthful. Be completely truthful in your application!**

If you have had trouble with the law in the past, provide complete details. Often applicants are refused not because of the offence, but because they fail to be completely truthful in their application. If you or a dependent family member has serious health problems, be sure to provide particulars. It is to your long-term advantage to provide complete details of your situation.

2

Sponsored Dependants (Family Class Relatives)

OVERVIEW OF THE PROCESS

This chapter deals only with Sponsored Dependants. If you determined in the previous chapter that you cannot apply in this category, please go on to Chapter 3. The process you will follow in your application as a Sponsored Dependant is very different from the one you would follow as an Independent Applicant. The Sponsored Dependant is the simplest category under which to emigrate.

The initial forms and interview

You should begin by asking your relative in Canada to contact the nearest Canada Immigration Centre. Your relative will then be given or sent certain forms to fill out. The forms will include an **Undertaking Of Assistance** and another form called a **Financial Evaluation**. A sponsoring guide will also be provided. Samples of both these forms and the instructions for their completion follow.

Your relative will complete these forms and mail them to the local Canadian Immigration Centre. Once approved, a copy of the Undertaking will be sent to the Canadian High Commission, Embassy or Consulate in your area of the world. You will be sent a letter by that office stating that an Undertaking of Assistance has been filed and approved in Canada and that you must now complete an **Application for Permanent Residence**. Once your completed application has been received by that office, a date and time will normally be set for you to meet an immigration officer.

Security and medical checks

After your interview, providing the immigration officer is satisfied with the results, a security check will be done on you and you will be asked to undergo a medical examination. This does not mean the immigration officer thinks you are sick or a subversive. These are routine checks done on every applicant, regardless of the immigration category in which you apply.

Once you have had your medical examination, the completed medical examination forms will be sent to Canadian immigration doctors by you or by the physician that examined you. You must be examined by a doctor in your country who is approved by the Canadian government to conduct such examinations.

Your immigration document

After the Canadian doctors have reviewed the results of the examination, they will transmit their decision back to the Immigration Office you are dealing with. Assuming you pass the medical examination and the security checks, you will then receive a document called an **Immigrant Visa and Record of Landing**. This is your 'immigrant visa' for Canada. You may then leave your country and travel to Canada as an immigrant.

Keep in mind that:

- You must enter Canada before the expiration date on the visa, which is usually some months from the date of issue.

- Visas will not be extended under any circumstances.

- There is no Canadian visa impressed in your passport.

- You must present your Immigrant Visa and Record of Landing to a Canadian immigration officer at the port of entry to Canada.

At the port of entry you will be asked to sign the Immigrant Visa and Record of Landing to verify the information it contains. The officer will record your entry and stamp your passport with a small stamp. You are then a permanent resident (**landed immigrant**) of Canada.

THE FORMS REQUIRED

The above description is only an overall picture of the process you will have to go through to become a landed immigrant through sponsorship by a close relative in Canada. I mentioned two forms your relative will have to fill out. Samples are included on the following pages, which reproduce a typical Sponsorship Kit provided by Immigration Offices in Canada.

Citizenship and   Citoyenneté et
Immigration Canada Immigration Canada

IMMIGRATION

Canada

Sponsoring a Family Class Relative

Spouse, dependent children,
fiancé(e), adopted children,
parents, grandparents

Table of Contents

Attachments:

Appendices:

   A Information for Canadian Citizens Living Exclusively Outside Canada

   B Sponsors Residing in Québec

   C Sponsoring an Adopted Child or a Child You Intend to Adopt

   D List of Provincial Contacts for Default Repayment of Social Assistance or Welfare

   E Population Chart

   F Low Income Cut-off Table

Forms:

Application to Sponsor a Member of the Family Class and Undertaking (IMM 1344A)

Financial Evaluation (IMM 1283)

Sponsorship Agreement (IMM 1344B)

Statutory Declaration of Common-Law Union (IMM 5409)

Document Checklist – Sponsor (IMM 5287)

Receipt (IMM 5401)

Cette trousse est également disponible en français

IMM 5196E (01–2000)

Canadä

Fig. 1.   Sponsorship Kit.

Important Information

If you need help with this application kit or you want to obtain another type of kit, please visit our web site at http://www.cic.gc.ca or phone a Call Centre. **The Call Centres are accessible only in Canada. If you live outside of Canada, refer to our web site.**

Call Centre Phone Numbers

If you reside in any of these areas, please call the local number

Montreal, serving the surrounding area	**(514) 496-1010**
Toronto, serving the Greater Toronto and Mississauga areas	**(416) 973-4444**
Vancouver, serving the Vancouver calling area	**(604) 666-2171**

For calls outside these areas, dial toll-free	**1-888-242-2100**

Using the Call Centre Service

The Call Centre is an automated system that can be accessed using a touch tone phone. The system can help answer some of your questions, order an application kit, or update you on the status of your case. It is available 24 hours a day. If you need to speak to an operator, you must call during normal working hours.

To access the automated service, dial the applicable number above. Have a pen and paper ready to record the information you receive. Select the language you want to use, either "1" for English or "2" for French. Next, select the service you want to use:

- Press "**1**" for Citizenship information
- Press "**2**" for Immigration information
- Press "**3**" to advise us of your change of address
- Press "**4**" for information on passports, birth certificates or other documents

Citizenship Application Kits

Citizenship Certificate (Proof of Citizenship)	Canadian Citizenship (Adults)
Canadian Citizenship (Minors)	Search of Citizenship Records

Immigration Application Kits

Changing Terms and Conditions or Extending Your Stay (Visitor, Student, Worker, Minister's Permit holder)	**Applying for Permanent Residence From Within Canada:**
Sponsoring a Family Class Relative	Spouses of Canadian Citizens or Permanent Residents
Refugee Sponsorship	Convention Refugee
Right of Landing Fee (ROLF) Loan	Humanitarian and Compassionate Cases
Request to Amend an Immigration Record of Landing	Live-in Caregiver
	Convention Refugee without Proper Identity Documents

> **This is not a legal document. For legal information, please refer to the *Immigration Act*, 1976 and *Immigration Regulations, 1978*.**

Overview

This kit contains all the forms and information to sponsor a Family Class relative. **Read all the instructions carefully before you begin.** If you do not meet **all** the sponsorship requirements outlined in the kit, you can expect that your relative's application will be refused. The processing fee will **not** be refunded.

Who can use this kit?

This kit can be used by:

- Canadian citizens or permanent residents who reside permanently in Canada and who want to sponsor a Family Class relative; or,
- Canadian citizens living exclusively outside Canada, who want to sponsor their spouse and dependent children under 19 and intend to return to Canada to live permanently with their family. See important instructions in Appendix A.
- Sponsors residing in Québec. See important information in Appendix B.

Who should not use this kit?

If you are a Canadian citizen with children born outside of Canada you may not need to sponsor them. Provided that you had Canadian citizenship when your child was born, you are not required to submit a sponsorship. Instead, you must apply for proof of citizenship for your child. To apply for a child in Canada, use the kit, Citizenship Certificate (Proof of Citizenship.) To apply for a child living outside of Canada, contact the Canadian embassy or consulate nearest to where he/she lives.

What does it mean to "sponsor?"

When you sponsor a Family Class relative, you sign a contract, called an **Undertaking**, with the Minister of Citizenship and Immigration (or with the Ministère des Relations avec les citoyens et de l'Immigration (MRCI) if you live in Quebec) promising to provide financial support for your relative's essential needs. The contract ensures that sponsored relatives do not have to apply for social assistance/ welfare. The contract is valid for 10 years (varies in Quebec) from the date your relatives become permanent residents.

Essential needs are food, clothing, shelter and other basic requirements for everyday living. Dental care, eye care and other health needs not covered by public health services are also included.

Who is a Family Class relative?

A Family Class relative is:

- your spouse to whom you are married. Your spouse must be a person of the opposite sex who is 16 years of age or older. The marriage must be legally recognized in the country where it took place;

- your fiancé(e);

- your dependent child (See definition below), including a child adopted before age 19;

- your parent or grandparent;

- your brother, sister, nephew, niece or grandchild who is an orphan, under age 19 and unmarried; and/or

- a dependent son or daughter whose adoption was finalized before having attained the age of 19, or a child under the age of 19 whom the sponsor intends to adopt and who is:

  - an orphan, (i.e. both parents deceased);

  - an abandoned child whose parents cannot be identified;

  - a child born outside of marriage who has been placed with a child welfare authority for adoption;

  - a child whose parents are separated and who has been placed with a child welfare authority for adoption; or

  - a child one of whose parents is deceased and who has been placed with a child welfare authority for adoption.

For more information on adoption cases, refer to Appendix C.

> **You may only sponsor a Family Class relative. You can expect that sponsorship applications for people who are not Family Class relatives will be refused. Processing fees will not be refunded.**

What is the definition of "dependent children?"

Dependent children may be your own or those of the relatives you are sponsoring. Dependent children:

a) are under the age of 19 and unmarried; or,

b) have been continuously enrolled and in attendance as full-time students in an educational institution and financially supported by their parents since turning 19 (or from the date of marriage if married before age 19.)

> **Students who interrupt their full-time studies continue to be considered dependents as long as they are not away from school for a total of more than one year and continue to be supported by parents during that time (school holidays need not be included); or,**

c) are unable to support themselves due to a medical condition and are financially supported by their parents.

> **Children included on the application must meet the definition of "dependent children" on the day the Case Processing Centre receives properly completed and signed sponsorship application forms and the correct processing fee. As well, dependent children described in a) must remain unmarried until they become permanent residents unless they meet the requirements in b).**

Can you sponsor another relative if you do not have any relatives listed above or any relatives who are Canadian citizens or permanent residents?

Yes, however, you must prove that you do not have a spouse, son, daughter, mother, father, brother, sister, grandparent, aunt, uncle, niece, or nephew who is a Canadian citizen or permanent resident and no family class relatives whom you could sponsor.

What are the requirements you must meet as a sponsor?

As a sponsor you must make sure that:

- your relative is a member of the Family Class (defined in **Who is a Family Class Relative?**);
- you are 19 years of age or older;
- you are a Canadian citizen or permanent resident;
- you physically reside in Canada

    Exception: Canadian citizens living exclusively outside of Canada may sponsor their spouse and unmarried children under the age of 19. If this describes your situation, see Appendix A for additional instructions.;

- you sign an **Undertaking** promising to provide for your relative and, if applicable, his/her spouse and dependent children's essential needs (defined previously in **What does it mean to sponsor?**) for 10 years;

- you provide us with documents that show your financial resources and obligations for the past 12 months;

- you meet the financial requirements explained in this kit; and,

- you and your relative sign a **Sponsorship Agreement** that confirms that each of you understands your mutual obligations and responsibilities.

You may **not** sponsor, if:

- relatives you sponsored in the past have received social assistance/welfare during the validity period of the sponsorship.

    If this is the case, you are considered to be in "default" of your sponsorship. You will not be able to sponsor anyone, including your spouse and children, until you repay the full amount of any social assistance/welfare payment or repay the debt to the satisfaction of the provincial or municipal authorities that issued the benefit. Contact the authorities in your province listed in Appendix D for more information on repayments.;

- you have not made a required payment on a transportation, assistance, or Right of Landing fee loan unless a collections officer has agreed to defer a payment. For information on your loan account call, 1-800-667-7301. You can only access this number if you live in Canada.);
- you are in prison; and/or,
- you are bankrupt.

You are a permanent resident of Canada, not a Canadian citizen; are there special requirements to sponsor?

Yes. If you:

- are under a removal order, do not send in your sponsorship application because it will be automatically refused.
- have been charged with a criminal offence where the courts could sentence you to a jail term of more than six months, your sponsorship application will not be dealt with until the court makes a final decision.
- have been convicted of a serious criminal offence, have provided false information to Immigration, or have not met conditions of entry, you may not be eligible to sponsor. If you mail your sponsorship application and there is a problem, the application may not be processed and you will lose the processing fee.

You do not have enough money to sponsor your relatives on your own; can someone co-sign your sponsorship application?

A sponsorship application may be co-signed by your spouse to whom you are legally married OR by a common-law spouse. A common-law spouse is a person of the opposite sex who has lived with you in a conjugal relationship for at least one year before the **Undertaking** is signed.

The co-signer must:

- Meet the same eligibility requirements as the sponsor, as listed in **What must you do as a sponsor?**;
- Agree to co-sign your application to sponsor your relatives; and,
- Agree to be responsible for your relatives' essential needs, as defined in **What does it mean to sponsor?**, for 10 years.

The co-signer will be equally liable if commitments are not met. If you are sponsoring a spouse or fiancé(e), you cannot have a co-signer.

Assets, potential earnings, or assistance from other family members will not be considered.

General Instructions

Before You Start

- Read all the instructions first.
- Photocopy the blank forms and use one as a working copy. Keep the working copy for your records.
- When completing the forms, print in large block letters with a black pen. Do not leave any questions on the forms unanswered.
- If you are sponsoring more than one family or part of a family (mother and/or father and dependent children), you must complete separate applications and receipts. Make photocopies of the application and order the correct number of receipts.

Examples:

a) You are sponsoring your mother and father and your spouse and dependent children. Complete one application and receipt for your parents and one application and receipt for your spouse and dependent children.

b) You are sponsoring two adopted children. Complete a separate application and receipt for each child.

c) You are sponsoring three orphaned brothers. Complete a separate application and receipt for each child.

WARNING! You (and, if applicable, your co-signer) must provide truthful and accurate information. The information provided may be verified. You can expect that processing will stop immediately if you or your co-signer give false or misleading information. It is a serious offence to make a false application.

Mailing Your Application

Once you (and, if applicable, your co-signer) have followed **all** the instructions in this kit and are certain you are eligible to apply, you may send your application to us. Send everything in a 23 cm x 30.5 cm (9" x 12") envelope. The envelope must be completed as follows:

Your Name
Your Address
Your Postal Code

Case Processing Centre
P.O. Box 6100, Station A
Mississauga, ON   L5A 4H4

- If this is an adoption case, please print "ADOPTION" above "Case Processing Centre."

The envelope will require more postage than a normal letter. To avoid having your application returned to you, have the Post office weigh it before mailing.

What if you need help?

If you still have questions after reading this kit, phone the nearest Call Centre or visit our web site. See page 2 for further information.

How to Complete the Forms

The following pages will help you (and, if applicable, your co-signer) fill in the forms included in this kit. It does not include instructions for all the boxes because most questions are clear; instructions are provided only when necessary.

 Application to Sponsor a Member of the Family Class and Undertaking (IMM 1344A)

A – Sponsor

The person who is directly related to the family members being sponsored must complete this section.

Box 7:   This may be a post office box, rural route number, or mailing address.

Box 14:   If applicable, write the date you became a permanent resident of Canada. The date is found in Box 45 of your *Immigrant Visa and Record of Landing* (IMM 1000.)

Box 15:   If you are a naturalized Canadian citizen and no longer have your *Immigrant Visa and Record of Landing* (IMM 1000), please print the name you used at the time you became a permanent resident.

Box 16:   You may choose a Canadian visa office where you want your sponsorship application to be sent. If you do not select a visa office, your sponsorship application will be sent to the visa office responsible for the area in which your relative lives.

- Sponsorships for relatives applying through the United States must be sent to the visa office in Buffalo. Sponsorships for relatives living in other countries cannot be sent to small satellite offices. Visit our web site for a list of visa offices.

- Choosing a visa office other than the one responsible for the area in which your relative lives may cause delays in the processing of your relative's application for permanent residence.

B – Co-signer

Your spouse or common-law spouse should complete this section only if he/she is co-signing the application. See the **Overview** section for information on co-signers.

If you are sponsoring a spouse or fiancé(e) leave this section blank.

Box 28 and 29: Follow the instructions for Box 14 and 15 above.

C – Family Members Being Sponsored and Their Dependents

(Attach a separate sheet if you need more space.)

Box 30:   If your relatives live in the People's Republic of China, you must print their names in pinyin.

- a) Print the last name of the relative you are sponsoring, the name before marriage (if applicable), and given names.

- b) If the relative you are sponsoring has a spouse who is accompanying him/her, print the person's first and last name in this section.

c) If the relative you are sponsoring or his/her spouse has dependent children who are accompanying him/her, print their first and last names in this section.

d) If the relative you are sponsoring has a spouse or dependent children who are NOT accompanying him/her, print their first and last names in this section.

Box 36:   For dependent children, put an "X" in Box A, B or C to indicate whether they are:

Type A: under age 19 and unmarried.

Type B: a full-time student and financially dependent on parents since turning 19 (or from the date of marriage if married before age 19.)

Students who interrupt their full-time studies continue to be considered dependents as long as they are not away from school for a total of more than one year and continue to be supported by parents during that time (school holidays need not be included.)

Type C: unable to support themselves due to a medical condition and are financially supported by their parents.

Box 37:   Print the **complete** address where your relative lives. If the relative is a young child, include the name of the person who will be looking after his/her mail.

Box 38:   If different from Box 37, print the mailing address where we can reach your relatives. Check the box if the address is the same as Box 37.

It is important that you give us a complete and correct address for your relatives or the application will be delayed.

D – Adoption Case

If you are sponsoring a child you have adopted or intend to adopt, refer to important information in **Appendix C**.

1. Check the appropriate box. If the child is already adopted, you must provide documentary evidence that you are the legal adoptive parents. See the **Document Checklist**.

2. Write the child's country of residence, or if the child is not yet identified, the country where you intend to adopt a child.

E – Sponsorship of a Fiancé(e)

If you are sponsoring your fiancé(e), read this section carefully. Keep the address for the Case Processing Centre in Mississauga listed in the **Mailing Your Application** section so that you can mail us the proof of marriage once you have married. Your fiancé(e) will make the same declaration when he/she applies for permanent residence.

F – Eligibility Assessment

This section must be completed by the sponsor (and, if applicable, the co-signer.) It will help determine if you are eligible to sponsor and if your spouse is eligible to co-sign the application.

If you find you are not eligible to sponsor or co-sign, do not send in your application because it will be refused and the processing fee will not be refunded.

Parts 1 and 2 to be Completed by Canadian Citizens and Permanent Residents

Part 1(c):   Your relative must be a member of the family class. See **Who is considered a Family Class relative?** in the **Overview** section of this kit.

Part 1(d):   You must physically live in Canada and continue to do so if your relatives receive permanent residence status.

Exception: Canadian citizens may submit a sponsorship for their spouse and unmarried children under the age of 19 if they are living exclusively outside of Canada. If this describes your situation, see Appendix A for additional instructions. Note: You must complete Section G – Residency Declaration.

Part 2(a):   If you have declared bankruptcy, do not submit this application unless you have been discharged from the bankruptcy.

Part 2(b):   Any relatives you have sponsored or for whom you have co-signed an application must not have received social assistance/welfare from any province or territory during the time you were responsible for them. If they have, do not submit your application unless you repay the full amount of any social assistance/welfare payments or repay the debt to the satisfaction of the provincial or municipal authorities that issued the benefit. For more information on how to repay the money, contact the responsible provincial department. (See **Appendix D**.)

Part 2(d):   Do not submit the sponsorship application if you have not made a required payment on a transportation, Right of Landing fee or assistance loan, unless you have made arrangements with a collections officer to defer payments. For further information on your loan account, contact 1-800-667-7301. You can only access this number if you live in Canada.

Part 2(e):   You may not sponsor anyone if you are in a jail, prison, penitentiary or reformatory. You may sponsor if you are on parole, probation, or are serving a suspended sentence.

Part 3 to be Completed by Permanent Residents Only

Part 3(a):   If you have been ordered to leave Canada, you will have received a written notice from us. If you are unsure if an outstanding order is in place, contact the nearest Call Centre to ask about your status. If you answer "yes," do not submit your application.

Part 3(b):   If you have been charged with a criminal offence, you may send in your application, however, we will not process it until the courts have made a decision on your case. If you are convicted of a serious offence, the application may be refused.

Part 3(c):   You may have violated Immigration law if you have been convicted of a serious criminal offence, have provided false information on previous applications or, have not met conditions of entry as a permanent resident. If you answer "yes," do not submit your application.

A serious offence means an offence for which the courts sentenced you to more than six months in prison or for which the courts could have imposed a sentence of five years or more.

G – Residency Declaration for Canadian Citizens Living Exclusively Outside of Canada

This section to be completed by Canadian citizens who are living exclusively outside of Canada and who are sponsoring a spouse and/or unmarried children under 19. See **Appendix A** for further information.

H – Consent

Privacy laws prevent us from discussing your application with anyone else unless you have given us permission. If you want us to release information about your application to someone else, print your representative's name in this section. If you would like all mail to be sent directly to your representative, write the person's address in this section.

If your representative is not a Canadian citizen or permanent resident, we cannot release information even with your permission.

I – Undertaking

Residents of all provinces and territories, except Québec, must read Section I.

Once the form is signed, the undertaking is a legal contract between you, your co-signer (if applicable), and the Minister of Citizenship and Immigration.

J – Declaration

Read this section carefully before signing Section K.

K– Signature(s)

You and, if applicable, your co-signer must sign this form. If you do not, your entire application will be returned to you and it will cause delays in processing.

Financial Evaluation (IMM 1283)

(Not applicable to residents of Québec.)

This form will help you assess if you (and, if applicable, your co-signer) will have the financial ability to support the relatives you are planning to sponsor.

You (and, if applicable, your co-signer) must prove that you have earned enough money over the last 12 months* to financially support:

- yourself;
- your dependents in Canada and elsewhere;
- your sponsored relatives including any dependents, whether or not these dependents are coming to Canada; and,
- any family members either you or, if applicable, your co-signer have sponsored before, where the undertaking is still valid.

* The Case Processing Centre will count the 12 month period immediately preceding the date they receive your complete and signed sponsorship application.

If you (and, if applicable, your co-signer) do not have enough money to support everyone listed above, you can expect that your application will be refused and that the processing fees will not be refunded.

If you are sponsoring your spouse and/or your dependent children who are under 19, unmarried and who have no children of their own, you do not need to meet the financial test. You must still complete this form. We will assess whether or not your spouse and children will be able to look after themselves financially without the need for social assistance.

Box 3:

Box 3A: Read and complete this section carefully. The total number of people who will depend on you for financial support, along with where you live, will determine the minimum money you will need to sponsor the relatives on this sponsorship application.

          Do not count a family member more than once.

          Example:

- If you previously sponsored your spouse, count him/her as someone you sponsored in the past (section vi), **not** as your spouse (section ii). If you are sponsoring your spouse on this application, count him/her in section iv), **not** as your spouse (section ii).

Box 3B: The amount of money that is required to sponsor relatives depends on the area in which you live.

1.   Find your place of residence in **Appendix E - Population Chart**. Determine whether your place of residence is described in category "A" or "B."

          If your place of residence is not described in the chart, go to the next section, "What if your community is not listed on the population chart?"

2.   Refer to **Appendix F - Low-Income Cut-off Table** and find the column that corresponds to the letter assigned to your place of residence. Go down the column until you come to the line that matches the number of people for whom you are responsible as determined in Box 3A. This is the amount of income you must have to sponsor your relatives.

Examples:

- You live in an area designated "A." You live in a place with a population size described in Column A. In **Box 3A**, you have determined that you are financially responsible for 7 people. You require an income of $44,339.

- You live in an area designated as "B." You live in a place with a population size described in Column B. In **Box 3A**, you have determined that you are financially responsible for 10 people. You require an income of $47,968.

3.   Write the amount of income you must have in **Box 3B**.

What if your community is not listed on the population chart?

1.   Contact your municipal government or City Hall to determine the population of your community.

2.   Refer to **Appendix F - Low-Income Cut-off Table** and find the column that corresponds to the population for your place of residence. Go down the column until you come to the line that matches the number of people for whom you are responsible as determined in Box 3A. This is the amount of income you must have to sponsor your relatives.

Example:

- You live in Kingston, Ontario which is not listed on the Population Chart. Kingston's population is between 100,000 and 499,000. You live in a place with a population size described in Column B. In **Box 3A**, you have determined that you are financially responsible for 7 people. You require an income of $38,032.

3.   Write the amount of income you must have in **Box 3B**.

Only income from Canadian sources that you (and, if applicable, your co-signer) have earned for the last 12 months can be used to determine if you have enough money to sponsor your relatives. The only exception is if you have received income from another country on which Canadian income tax has been paid. You must provide proof of all income. See the Document Checklist.

Box 4:   Print the required employer and/or self-employment (business or professional) information. Use the following definitions:

- **Employment Income:** The gross income earned from your job(s) as reported to Revenue Canada from a T4.

- **Business Income:** The gross income earned and reported to Revenue Canada from activities conducted for profit from a sole proprietorship, partnership or unincorporated business. This would include professions, trades and businesses such as small retail outlets and restaurants.

- **Self-employment Earnings:** The gross income earned and reported to Revenue Canada from self-employment endeavours such as farming, fishing, commission sales, consulting and childcare that are conducted for profit.

Box 5:   Your spouse or common-law spouse should complete this section if he/she is co-signing the sponsorship application. Print the required employer and/or self-employment (business or professional) information. Use the definitions above.

Box 6:   If you have a co-signer, calculate the total employment income amount by adding Box 4 and Box 5. If you do not have a co-signer, enter the amount from Box 4.

Box 7:   Calculate income that you (and, if applicable, your co-signer) have from other sources. Use the following definitions for Box 7:

- **Rental Income:** Income earned and reported to Revenue Canada from rental property.

- **Investment and Interest Income:** Income reported to and accepted by Revenue Canada from dividend payments, interest, stocks, bonds and other investments and, interest on savings deposits.

- **Maternity/Parental/Sickness Benefits:** Only maternity, parental and sickness benefits paid under the *Employment Act* are considered income. Other payments such as Employment Insurance and federal training allowances are NOT considered as income.

- **Pension Income:** Income from Old Age Security, Canada/Quebec Pension Plan, other pensions, superannuation and annuity payments from Canadian sources. Do not include Guaranteed Income Supplement (GIS) payments.

- **Other income:** Include income you have received and will continue to receive on a regular basis that is not included above, (e.g. alimony, child support). Please specify the source of the income on the form.

You cannot include provincial training allowances, social assistance, child tax benefits, or Employment Insurance payments.

Box 8: Add Box 6 and 7C. This amount is your total income available.

Box 9: Calculate your (and, if applicable, your co-signer's) debts and financial obligations. For each item, print the total payments you made over the past 12 months. Print the total of all items in Box 9C.

You must report your business expenses and personal obligations separately.

Use the following definitions to help you fill in this section:

- **Mortgages on principal residence:** Total payments made on second, third and other mortgages on your principal residence. Do **NOT** include first mortgages.

- **Rents and mortgages on non-principal residences:** All rental and mortgage payments (including first and other mortgages) for properties other than your principal residence, (e.g. cottages, rental properties, etc.). Do **NOT** include rent for your principal residence.

- **Property and school taxes:** Payments made to school boards or municipalities on all properties that you own. Do not include taxes that you have included as part of your business or rental expenses.

- **Personal loans and lines of credit:** Negotiated payments made or still due on loans and/or lines of credit at a bank, trust company or other lender.

- **Student loans:** Total payments made or still due on student loan(s.)

- **Immigration loans:** Payments made or still due on transportation loans, Right of Landing fee loans, and other assistance loans from Canada Immigration.

- **All other loans:** Payments made or that are still due on loans not listed above.

- **Business expenses:** Total business expenses that are deductible under the *Income Tax Act.*

- **Rental expenses:** Total expenses related to rental expenses that are deductible under the *Income Tax Act.*

- **Investment expenses:** Expenses related to investing.

- **Interest due on Credit cards:** Total interest paid or still due on all credit cards. (VISA, MasterCard, department stores, other business credit cards, etc.)
- **Alimony Payments:** Do **not** include alimony payments if you have counted your former spouse in Box 3A.
- **Court-directed payments:** Money paid as a result of a court order, e.g. defaulted loan payments.

  Do **not** include child support payments if you have included your children in Box 3A.
- **Income tax payments on arrears:** Payments made to Revenue Canada for reassessments or previously unpaid taxes not paid by April 30th of the corresponding tax year.
- **Insurance payments:** Payments for disability, life, home, business or other insurance. Do not include payments for business matters that you have included as a business expense.
- **Other:** Other payments made or due over the last 12 months.

Box 10: Subtract the number in Box 9C from the number in Box 8. This is the amount of money that you (and, if applicable, your co-signer) have available to sponsor.

Box 11: Print the amount that is written in Box 3B. If the amount in Box 10 is equal to or greater than the number in Box 11, you likely have enough money to support the number of relatives in Box 3A.

> **If the amount in Box 10 is less than Box 11, submit your sponsorship application only if you are sponsoring your spouse and/or your dependent children who are under age 19, unmarried, and who have no dependent children of their own.**

Sponsorship Agreement (IMM 1344B)

(Not applicable to residents of Québec.)

Read the form carefully. Follow these steps:

1.   You (and, if applicable, your co-signer,) sign the form.

2.   Have the relative you are sponsoring sign the form.

   To save time, you can fax it to your relative outside of Canada, have him/her sign it and fax it back to you.

3.   Once your relative has signed the form, make two photocopies.

4.   Give one photocopy to your relative and send one to us. You must keep the original in a safe place.

   An agreement is not required if the relative you are sponsoring is under 19 and is NOT a spouse or fiancé(e).

Can anyone sign the agreement on behalf of your sponsored relative?

No. The applicant's signature is required.

> **You are not eligible to sponsor unless there is a completed agreement with your application. If you do not include the signed agreement with the other required documents and forms, you can expect that your application will be refused.**

Statutory Declaration Of Common-law Union (IMM 5409)

Complete this form only if you and your co-signer are in a common-law relationship. See the **Overview** section for the definition of a common-law spouse and information on co-signers.

A Commissioner for Oaths must certify this document. Provincial laws govern who can act in this position. In general, Members of Legislative Assemblies (MLAs), judges, justices of the peace, and lawyers are authorized to take oaths. Check your phone book for listings.

Send the original form with your sponsorship application.

How to Pay the Immigration Fees

This section explains how and where to pay immigration fees.

Exception: Canadian citizens living exclusively outside of Canada, who are sponsoring their spouse and unmarried children under the age of 19, must follow the fee payment instructions in Appendix A.

What fees are required?

You must pay a **Processing Fee** when you submit your sponsorship application and a **Right of Landing Fee** before the application for permanent residence of your relative can be finalized. If you pay the Right of Landing Fee when you submit your application, it will facilitate the handling of the application as we will not have to contact you later. If you do not do so, you will be asked to pay this fee when the visa office abroad is ready to issue the Immigrant Visa. Failure to pay the fee promptly when requested will result in a delay in the finalization of the application.

Processing Fees:

* $500 for each person who is a spouse or a fiancé/fiancée (of any age) and any other person 19 years of age or older, and
* $100 for any other person under age 19 and unmarried

Right of Landing Fee:

* $975 for each person 19 years of age or older

Are fees refundable?

Processing Fees

Once the Case Processing Centre has started processing the application, the processing fee will not be refunded, regardless of the final decision.

After you have read this guide, you should be able to decide whether you are eligible to sponsor a relative and if you have the required income, information and documentation for the application to be approved. Make sure that you are eligible before you pay your fees and that you provide all the information requested before you submit the application for processing. If you are found not to be eligible to sponsor your relatives, the processing fee will not be refunded.

If you apply again, you will have to pay another processing fee.

Right of Landing Fee

The Right of Landing fee will be refunded if the applicant is refused (i.e., by the visa office, Appeals, or upon receipt of a written request to withdraw) or if your relative is not granted permanent resident status. If you are entitled to a refund, you should receive it 4 to 6 weeks after the refund request has been completed by the Case Processing Centre.

How do you calculate the correct amount of fees required?

Step 1: Use this chart to calculate the fees required.

A	PROCESSING FEES	Number of Persons	Amount per Person	Amount Due
Spouse or fiancé/fiancée of any age **and** any other applicant 19 years of age or older			x $500	
Any other person under age 19 and unmarried			x $100	
			Total A	**$**

Complete this portion if you have decided to pay the Right of Landing fee with your application. The Right of Landing fee must be paid before landing will be granted. If this fee is paid with the application we will not have to contact you later.

B	RIGHT OF LANDING FEE	Number of Persons	Amount per Person	Amount Due
Any person 19 years of age and older			x $975	
			Total B	**$**
			Total fees paid (A+B)	**$**

Step 2: Verify your calculations.

Step 3: Fill out one receipt form (IMM 5401) per application.

An original receipt must be used; **a photocopy is not acceptable.** You can order an original receipt from our web site at http://www.cic.gc.ca, or contact a Call Centre agent.

Step 4 Insert the 'Total' on line 09 (Immigration Services Fees) of the receipt.

Do **not** complete the upper two parts of the receipt. These will be completed by the financial institution.

Step 5 Complete the Payer information sections on the reverse of the receipt.

Step 6 Bring the receipt and your payment to the financial institution.

Do **not** make payment using the automated teller machines.

What if you make an incorrect payment?

If you are required to pay additional fees, the Case Processing Centre will send you a form (IMM 5412) which will indicate the amount required for correct payment. Not paying the correct fee will result in a delay in finalizing your application. This payment must also be paid at a designated financial institution.

If you have paid too much, your application will be processed and the amount of the overpayment will be refunded. A cheque will be issued by Citizenship and Immigration Canada as soon as possible.

Who can pay the fees?

Anyone can pay the fees.

Where can the fees be paid?

Payment can be made at most financial institutions in Canada. Check with financial institutions in your area.

Note: There is no banking charge to pay. The service is free.

What can you use to pay the fees?

The financial institution will let you know what form of payment it considers acceptable. Please note that personal cheques and traveller's cheques are not acceptable.

What if there is no local financial institution which will accept payment?

In this situation, you may pay the fees by mail. Call a Call Centre for instructions.

What does the financial institution do?

The financial institution will accept your payment. The financial institution will stamp and insert the amount paid in the upper two portions of the receipt. You will receive the top two portions of the receipt. **Make sure you are given these and that they have been stamped and completed before you leave the financial institution.**

Note: Do not present your application to the financial institution, only your receipt.

What do you do after you have paid the fees?

Retain the top portion (Copy 1 – Client's copy) of the receipt which you have been given for your records. Attach the middle portion (Copy 2 – To be sent by client to Citizenship and Immigration Canada) to your completed application and mail it to the Case Processing Centre.

Note: Do not send any other form of payment with your application.

Using the Document Checklist (IMM 5287)

The **Document Checklist** helps to ensure that you attach all required documents to your sponsorship application. If any information is missing, your application will be returned to you.

Enclose the Document Checklist with your application.

Frequently Asked Questions

What if you move?

Phone the Call Centre immediately with your complete address. For Canadian citizens living exclusively abroad, write to the Case Processing Centre.

Should you hire a lawyer or consultant?

You are free to hire a lawyer or consultant to help you with your application; however, it is not necessary if you follow the instructions in this application kit.

Faster or more favourable processing is not given to people with representatives. If you hire a representative, he/she cannot claim faster service or a more favourable outcome.

What happens after your sponsorship application is reviewed?

You will:

- receive a letter within 8 weeks advising you whether or not your sponsorship application has been approved.
- receive a package, sent separately from the above letter, with instructions and application forms (*Immigrant Application Form [Application for Permanent Residence in Canada]* IMM 0008) that your relatives outside Canada must complete. You will have to send this package to your relatives living outside of Canada.

The Case Processing Centre will:

- send a copy of your sponsorship forms to the Canadian visa office responsible for the area in which your relatives live, unless you have specified another office on the *Application to Sponsor a Member of the Family* and *Undertaking* form.

> **No further processing will take place until the visa office receives a completed application for permanent residence from your relative.**

What happens after the visa office receives the application for permanent residence forms and the sponsorship forms?

Your relatives:

- will have to prove their relationship to you by sending in birth certificates, marriage certificates, etc.;
- will have to pass an immigration medical examination;
- will have to pass criminal and security checks conducted by the visa office;
- will have to obtain passports and, in some countries, exit visas; and,
- may have to go for an interview.

The visa office:

- may reassess whether or not you are able to fulfill the sponsorship obligations; and,
- will approve or refuse your relatives' applications for permanent residence.

> **Your relatives should not quit their jobs or sell their assets until they have their immigrant visas.**

When will your relatives outside of Canada get their visas?

Your relatives will receive a letter from the visa office advising of estimated processing times.

Can you cancel your undertaking?

If you change your mind about sponsoring your relatives, you must write a letter to the Case Processing Centre in Mississauga and the visa office **before** your relatives are issued immigrant visas. The processing fees will not be refunded. If immigrant visas were already issued, the promise you made to support your family for 10 years (varies in Quebec) will be valid.

What if your co-signer withdraws his/her financial support?

If your spouse or common-law spouse withdraws support for the sponsorship application, you or your spouse must write a letter to the Case Processing Centre in Mississauga and the visa office **before** immigrant visas are issued. You must include an amended copy of the sponsorship applications and agreement, initialed by you and you co-signer, removing the co-signer's support. We will assess your financial situation to see if you have enough money to support your family without a co-signer. If you do not meet the financial requirements on your own, your relatives' application for permanent residence may be refused.

Why might your relatives' application for permanent residence be refused?

There are many possible reasons why an application for permanent residence might be refused. Some examples are:

- you may not meet the financial requirements;
- your relatives may not have provided the required documents as requested by the visa office;
- the relationship between you and your family member is for convenience only. For example, you married your spouse to bring him/her to Canada but do not intend to live together; or,
- your relative has a criminal record or serious illness.

The visa office will write your relatives a letter and let them know why the application was refused.

If there is a refusal, do you have the right to appeal the decision?

Yes. If your relatives' application for permanent residence is refused, you will be informed in writing of your right to appeal by the visa office that processed their case. Follow the instructions in the letter that is sent to you. The Immigration Appeal Division will review your appeal.

Appendix A
Information For Canadian Citizens Living Exclusively Outside Canada

If you live exclusively outside of Canada, you can qualify to sponsor if you are a Canadian citizen who is sponsoring your **spouse** and/or **unmarried children who are under the age of 19 and have no dependent children of their own**. If you are travelling as a tourist, you are not considered to be residing abroad.

If this describes your situation follow these instructions:

1. Read the following sections in this kit and complete the forms:

   - **Overview**

   - **General Instructions**

     Read only the Before You Start section.

   - **How to Complete the Forms**

     For the *Financial Evaluation* (IMM 1283) form complete only boxes 1, 2, 3A, 4, 7 and sign the form.

   - **Using the Document Checklist**

     For proof of income, only include a letter from your current employer or bank statements.

2. Pay the Immigration fees as described below:

   Step 1:   Read the sections in the kit concerning the required fees and refund policy. Use the chart to calculate the fees.

   Step 2:   Obtain an international bank draft or money order, payable to the Receiver General for Canada, for the required amount in Canadian funds. Ensure that the bank draft or money order can be cashed through a Canadian financial institution.

   Step 3:   Include the bank draft or money order with your completed sponsorship application.

3. Mail your sponsorship:

   Unless you have received alternate instructions from a visa office outside of Canada, mail your application to the Case Processing Centre. P.O. Box 6100, Station A, Mississauga, ON, L5A 4H4, Canada.

4. Provide the following additional information:

   Include information showing that you intend to live in Canada with your spouse and/or children once they receive their immigrant visas and permanent residence status, e.g. offer of employment from a Canadian employer.

Appendix B
Sponsors Residing In Quebec

An agreement reached between the federal and Quebec governments gives the province responsibility for determining whether or not sponsors residing in Quebec have the financial ability to sponsor family members.

If you reside in Quebec, you must read the information and follow the general instructions in this kit. However, you only have to complete one form, specifically, *Application to Sponsor a Member of the Family Class and Undertaking* (IMM1344A).

The *Ministère des Relations avec les citoyens et de l'Immigration* of the Quebec government (MRCI), will send you other documents to complete, including an undertaking application form (*Demande d'engagement*).

If you want to sponsor a family member other than your spouse or children under 19 years of age, you, and if applicable, your co-signer, will have to prove to the MRCI that you have sufficient income to provide for the essential needs of:

- yourself;
- your dependants in Canada or elsewhere;
- the person you are sponsoring and his/her dependants, whether or not they are coming to Canada; and,
- the family members either you and, if applicable, your co-signer have sponsored before, where the undertakings are still in effect.

You and, if applicable, your co-signer must also meet the following MRCI requirements:

- have earned sufficient income over the last 12 months; and,
- prove that you have a steady income.

MRCI may reject a sponsorship application if:

- you and, if applicable, your co-signer have not fulfilled a previous sponsorship obligation because the person you sponsored received social assistance (last resort benefits), unless you have repaid the money to the Quebec government;
- during the last five years, you or your co-signer have failed to provide support payment obligations (alimony) for a child or former spouse.

To help you decide if you have the financial ability to sponsor your family members, we are providing the income scale in effect in Québec from January 1 to December 31, 1999. These amounts are indexed each year. We encourage you to use the Québec Income Scale to determine your financial ability to meet sponsorship requirements. Note that your calculations will only be an estimate since an MRCI employee will make the official financial assessment.

Québec Income Scale, 2000

Basic Needs of Sponsor and Dependent Persons	
Number of dependent persons	**Gross annual income of sponsor**
0	$16,632
1	$22,453
2	$27,720
3	$31,879
4	$35,482
Required gross annual income is increased by $3,603 for each additional dependent.	

Basic Needs of Sponsored Persons		
Persons 18 and over	**Persons under 18**	**Annual gross amount required by sponsor**
0	1	$5,757
0	2	$9,125
The annual gross amount required is increased by $3,042 for each additional person under 18.		
1	0	$12,166
1	1	$16,347
1	2	$18,456
The annual gross amount required is increased by $2,109 for each additional person under 18.		
2	0	$17,840
2	1	$19,986
2	2	$21,573
The annual gross amount required is increased by $1,585 for each additional person under 18 and by $5,673 for each additional person 18 or over.		

Example:	
Basic needs of a sponsor: (sponsor, spouse and 2 minor children)	$31,879
Basic needs of sponsored person: (main sponsored persons, spouse, 1 child of major age and 2 minor children)	$27,246
Income necessary to acceptance of undertaking application	**$59,125**

If you think you meet the MRCI's financial requirements, fill out the sponsorship application according to the instructions in this kit and send it, with the fees and supporting documents, to the Case Processing Centre.

The Case Processing Centre will review your application for sponsorship and send it to the MRCI. When the MRCI receives your application, they will send you an undertaking kit. Be sure to follow the instructions. Once you have filled out the forms, return them, together with the requested documents, to the MRCI. The MRCI will let you know whether your undertaking has been accepted or refused. The person you are sponsoring should include a copy of this decision with the application for permanent residence that he/she sends to the Canadian visa office abroad.

Please note that processing fees for sponsorship applications and undertakings are not, under any circumstances, refundable.

For further information on MRCI requirements, please contact your nearest regional office.

Direction régionale de Montréal
415 rue Saint-Roch
Montréal, Québec
H3N 1K2
(514) 864-9191

Bureau de Jonquière
3950 boul. Harvey
Jonquière, Québec
G7X 8L6
(418) 695-8144

Bureau de Trois-Rivières
100 rue Laviolette, 1er étage
Trois-Rivières, Québec
G9A 5S9
(819) 371-6011 ou
1 888 879-4294

Direction régionale de la Montérégie
2533 rue Cartier
Longueuil, Québec
J4K 4G5
(450) 928-7783

Direction régionale de Québec
890 avenue de Lévis
Québec, Québec
G1S 3E1
(418) 643-1435 ou
1 888 643-1435

Direction régionale de l'Estrie
740 rue Galt ouest, bureau 400
Sherbrooke, Québec
J1H 1Z3
(819) 820-3606 ou
1 888 879-4288

Direction régionale de l'Outaouais
259 boul. Saint-Joseph, bureau 101
Hull, Québec
J8Y 6T1
(819) 772-3021
1 888 295-9095

Direction régionale de Laval – Laurentides – Lanaudière
800 boul. Chomedey, Tour C, Bureau 200
Laval, Québec
H7V 3Y4
(514) 681-2593 ou
1 800 375-7426

Appendix C
Sponsoring an Adopted Child or a Child You Intend to Adopt

This appendix provides only basic information. For more details refer to the booklet *International Adoption and the Immigration Process* available from our Call Centres at the phone numbers listed on page 2.

As adoption is a provincial responsibility, people who wish to adopt a child from outside of Canada must first contact provincial/territorial adoption authorities. Addresses are available in the booklet named above. Once you have initiated the adoption application through the provincial/territorial authorities and have obtained the appropriate approval, you may begin the sponsorship process for a child described below:

- For adoptions completed abroad, the child must be under age 19 and adopted according to the laws of the country of origin.

- For adoptions completed abroad or in Canada, the child must be under age 19; and,

  - an orphan;

  - an abandoned child whose parents cannot be identified; OR,

  - a child placed with a child welfare authority for adoption because he or she was born outside of marriage, has parents who have separated, or has only one living parent.

Sponsorships for children who are not yet identified are accepted; once the child is identified, it is the sponsor's responsibility to notify the appropriate visa office and provincial authority. For Québec residents, please contact the office of the *Ministère des Relations avec les citoyens et de l'Immigration* for sponsorship requirements in Québec. (See Appendix B for phone numbers.)

If a sponsorship is approved, an application for permanent residence must be submitted. (Instructions will be given at the time of approval.) Generally, an application for permanent residence will be approved if the child passes an Immigration medical examination and if a visa officer is satisfied that the adoption will create a genuine parent-child relationship. It will not be approved if a visa officer concludes that the purpose of the adoption is to gain admission for the child or the child's relatives.

For all adoption cases, there is an immigration requirement prior to visa issuance to obtain a letter from the provincial/territorial authorities stating that they have no objection to the proposed arrangements for reception and care of the child. Immigration will make this request directly to the appropriate provincial/territorial authorities at the time of the sponsorship approval.

The Hague Convention on Intercountry Adoption (as of april 16, 1999)

Depending on which province/territory you live in and where the adoption will take place, the process may also be subject to the Hague Convention on Inter-Country Adoptions. You must initiate your adoption application through the provincial/territorial adoption authority and obtain the appropriate approval for adoption. For provincial/territorial contacts, refer to the booklet *International Adoption and Immigration Process*. The Hague Convention will apply if you live in one of the following provinces/territories::

Alberta	New Brunswick	Prince Edward Island
British Columbia	Nova Scotia	Saskatchewan
Manitoba	Ontario	Yukon

and intend to adopt a child from one of the following countries:

Andorra	Costa Rica	Lithuania	Paraguay
Australia	Cyprus	Mauritius	Peru
Austria	Denmark	Mexico	Philippines
Brazil	Ecuador	Moldova	Poland
Burkina Faso	El Salvador	Monaco	Romania
Burundi	Finland	Netherlands	Spain
Canada	France	New Zealand	Sri Lanka
Chile	Georgia	Norway	Sweden
Colombia	Israel	Panama	Venezuela

Other countries and provinces/territories may be added to this list at any time. Contact a provincial/territorial adoption authority or Call Centre to verify that this is the most recent list.

Appendix D
List of Provincial Contacts

This list of provincial contacts is for sponsors who need information on how to repay money for defaults on previous sponsorships

The following offices can only answer questions about repayment of money on defaulted sponsorships. They cannot answer questions about other immigration issues.

British Columbia
Ministry of Social Development
and Economic Security
Sponsorship Default Co-ordinator
2280 Kingsway
Vancouver, BC V5N 5M9
1 (604) 660-5350

Alberta
Department of Family and Social Services
Income and Employment Programs
Employment and Training Initiatives
14th Floor, Seventh Street Plaza
10030 – 107 Street
Edmonton, AB T5J 3E4
1 (780) 427-2619

Saskatchewan
Saskatchewan Social Services
1920 Broad Street, 11th Floor
Regina, SK S3P 3V6
1 (306) 787-3494

Manitoba
Department of Family Services
114 Garry Street, Room 305
Winnipeg, MB R3C 4V7
1 (204) 945-2177

Ontario
Ministry of Community and Social Services
7th Floor, Hepburn Block
80 Grosvenor Street
Toronto, ON M7A 1E9
1 (416) 325-5666

Québec
Ministère de l'emploi et de la solidarité
415 St. Roch, local 1.11
Montréal, QC H3N 1K2
1 (514) 873-6904

Newfoundland
Department of Social Services
P.O. Box 8700
St. John's, NF A1B 4J6
1 (709) 729-0583

New Brunswick
Department of Human Resource Development
P.O. Box 6000
Fredericton, NB E3B 5H1
1 (506) 453-2712

Nova Scotia
Department of Community Services
P.O. Box 696
Halifax, NS B3J 2T7
1 (902) 424-4262

Prince Edward Island
Department of Health and Social Services
11 Kent Street, 2nd Floor
P.O. Box 2000
Charlottetown, PEI C1A 7N8
1 (902) 368-4900

Appendix E
Population Chart

If you live in an area that is adjacent to or near the following cities, you are likely part of an area known as a "Census Metropolitan Area." This is a large urban area that includes a city and any adjacent areas (towns, municipalities, rural areas) that have a high degree of social and economic integration.

Census Metropolitan Area				Category
Calgary, Alberta and surrounding area, including:				
Airdrie	Cochrane	Delacour	Keith	
Balzac	Conrich	Gayford	Keoma	
Beiseker	Crossfield	Inverlake	Langdon	A
Bragg Creek	Dalemead	Irricana	Radnor	
Chestermere	Dalroy	Kathryn	Sarcee	
Edmonton, Alberta and surrounding area, including:				
Acheson	Duffield	Josephburg	Point Alison	
Akenside	Edmonton Beach	Kapasiwin	Redwater	
Alcomdale	Elk Island	Kavanagh	Rolly View	
Alexander Reserve	Ellerslie	Keephills	Seba Beach	
Ardrossan	Entwistle	Lamoureux	Sherwood Park	
Antross	Excelsior	Lancaster Park	Spruce Grove	
Beaumont	Fallis	Leduc	St. Albert	
Betula Beach	Fedorah	Leduc County 25	Stony Plain	
Bon Accord	Fort Saskatchewan	Legal	Strathcona County	
Bremner	Gainford	Lindbergh	Sturgeon County	A
Bruderheim	Genesee	Looma	Sundance Beach	
Calmar	Gibbons	Magnolia	Telfordville	
Cannell	Glen Park	Matthew's Crossing	Thorsby	
Carbondale	Golden Days	Moon Lake	Tomahawk	
Cardiff	Golden Spike	Morinville	Val Soucy	
Carvel	Good Hope	Namao	Villeneuve	
Cooking Lake	Graminia	New Serepta	Wabumun	
Deville	Griesbach	Nisku	Warburg	
Devon	Huggett	Parkland County	Whitecroft	
Duagh	Itaska Beach	Pembina	Winterburn	
Halifax, Nova Scotia and surrounding area, including:				
Antrim	Ferguson Cove	Kinsac	Oldham	
Bald Rock	Fernleigh	Lake Echo	Parkdale	
Bayside	French Village	Lake Egmont	Peggy's Cove	
Bear Cove	Frenchmans Road	Lakeside	Pockwock	
Bedford	Gaetz Brook	Lakeview	Porters Lake	
Blind Bay	Glen Haven	Lantz	Portobello	
Boutiliers Point	Glen Margaret	Lawrencetown	Portuguese Cove	
Carrolls Corner	Goffs	Lewis Lake	Preston	
Cole Harbour	Grand Lake	Lloy	Princes Lodge	
Cooks Brook	Greenwood Heights	Lower Prospect	Prospect	
Cow Bay	Grono Road	Lucasville	Queensland	B
Dartmouth	Halibut Bay	Masons Point	Rainbow Haven	
Devils Island	Hatchet Lake	McGraths Cove	Sackville	
East Chezzetcook	Hubbard's	McNab Island	Sandy Cove	
East Dover	Hubley	Meaghers Grant	Seabright	
East Pennant	Humber Park	Melville Cove	Seaforth	
Eastern Passage	Indian Harbour	Micmac	Shannon Park	
Elderbank	Indian Point	Middle Village	Shearwater	
Elmsdale	Ingramport	Millview	Sheldrake Lake	
Enfield	Jollimore	Mineville	Sherwood Heights	
English Corner	Kent Park	Musquodoboit	Shubenacadie	
Fall River	Ketch Harbour	Oakfield	South East Passage	
			(continued)	

· Census Metropolitan Area				Category
Halifax, Nova Scotia and surrounding area, including: (continued)				
Southdale	Todds Island	West Dover	Windsor Junction	
Springfield Lake	Tufts Cove	West Pennant	Woodlawn	
Stillwater Lake	Umlah Point	Westphal	Woodside	**B**
Terence Bay	Waverly	Whites Lake	Wrights Cove	
Terminal Beach	Wellington	Wildwood Lake	Wyses Corner	
Three Fathom Harbour	West Chezzetcook	Williamswood	Yankeetown	
Hamilton, Ontario and surrounding area, including:				
Alberton	Copetown	Hannon	Stoney Creek	
Aldershot	Dundas	Jerseyville	Tapleytown	
Ancaster	Elfrida	Lynden	Troy	
Ash	Flamborough	Mount Hope	Vinemount	
Binbrook	Freelton	Peters Corners	Waterdown	**A**
Burlington	Fruitland	Rockton	West Flamborough	
Carlisle	Glanbrook	Rosedale	Westover	
Carluke	Greensville	Sheffield	Winona	
Cedar Springs	Grimsby	St. John's		
Kitchener–Waterloo, Ontario and surrounding area, including:				
Ayr	Centreville	Erbsville	St. Jacobs	
Bloomingdale	Clyde	Floradale	West Montrose	
Branchton	Conestogo	Heidelberg		**B**
Breslau	Doon	Maryhill		
Cambridge	Elmira	Roseville		
London, Ontario and surrounding area, including:				
Arva	Devizes	Lambeth	Shedden	
Belmont	Dorchester	Medway Heights	Sparta	
Chelsea Green	Eden	Mossley	St. Thomas	**B**
Cherry Grove	Glanworth	Port Stanley	Talbotville Royal	
Delaware	Hyde Park	Putnam	Thorndale	
Denfield	Komoka	Sharon	Union	
Oshawa, Ontario and surrounding area, including:				
Ashburn	Enniskillen	Mount Carmel	Raglan	
Bowmanville	Hampton	Myrtle	Tyrone	
Brooklin	Haydon	Newtonville	Whitby	**B**
Clarington	Kirby	Orono		
Columbus	Maple Grove	Port Darlington		
Ottawa, Ontario and surrounding area (not including Hull, Québec):				
Antrim	Cumberland	Greely	Malwood	
Ashton	Cyrville	Grenfell Glen	Manion Corners	
Baxters Corners	Dalmeny	Hammond	Manotick	
Becketts Creek	Davidson Corner	Harwood Plains	Marathon	
Becketts Landing	Deschénes	Herbert Corners	Marchhurst	
Bells Corners	Dirleton	Hiawatha Park	Metcalfe	
Berrys	Dwyer Hill	Huntley	Mills Corners	
Cambrian Heights	Eaglesons Corners	Ironside	Mohrs Corners	
Canaan	Edwards	Jockvale	Munster	
Cardinal Heights	Ellwood	Johnston Corners	Navan	
Carp	Elm	Kanata	Nepean	
Carlsbad Springs	Enniskerry	Kars	North Gower	**A**
Carsonby	Ettyville	Kempark	Orient	
Casselman	Federal	Kenmore	Orleans	
Cheney	Fitzroy	Kilmaurs	Osgoode	
City View	French Hill	Kinburn	Panmure	
Clarence	Galetta	Laurentian View	Pine Glen	
Clearview	Glen Cairn	Leitrim	Piperville	
Constance Bay	Gleneagle	Leonard	Reevecraig	
Corkery	Gloucester	Limbour	Richmond	
Crestview	Goodstown	Lynhurst	Rideau	
Crystal Bay	Goulbourn	MacLaren's Landing	Riviera	
			(continued)	

Census Metropolitan Area				Category

Ottawa, Ontario and surrounding area (not including Hull, Québec): (continued)

Rockcliffe Park	St. Pascal	Twin Elm	Vydon Acres	
Rockland	Stanley Corners	Vanier	Watterson Corners	
Russell	Stapledon	Vars	Woodlawn	**A**
Sarsfield	Stittsville	Vernon		
Shirleys Bay	Strathearn	Victory Hill		
Spring Hill	Talon	Vinette		

Regina, Saskatchewan and surrounding area, including:

Balgonie	Dreghorn	Grand Coulee	Pilot Butte	
Belle Plaine	Eastview	Jameson	Regina Beach	
Buena Vista	Edenwold	Lumsden	Wascana	**B**
Condie	Emerald Park	Lumsden Beach	White City	
Disley	Frankslake	Pense		

Saint John, New Brunswick and surrounding area, including:

Acamac	Erbs Cove	Ketepec	Quinton Heights	
Anthonys Cove	Evandale	Kingston	Quispamis	
Bains Corner	Fairfield	Lakewood Heights	Randolph	
Barnesville	Fairvale	Lepreau	Red Head	
Baxters Corner	Five Fathom Hole	Linley	Reeds Point	
Belmont	Forest Hills	Long Reach	Renforth	
Black Beach	French Village	Lorneville	Riverview Heights	
Black Point	Frenchman Creek	Lynch Corner	Rothesay	
Black River	Gardner Creek	Maces Bay	Sagwa	
Blagdon	Garnett	Martinon	Saint Martin	
Blairs	Glen Falls	Midwood	Salina	
Blindman Lake	Glenwood	Milford	Salmon River	
Bowes Lake	Golden Grove	Milkish	Seaview	
Bradley Lake	Gondola Point	Milledgeville	Shanklin	
Brookville	Gorhams Bluff	Mink Brook	Sherwood Park	
Browns Corner	Grand Bay	Mispec	Silver Falls	
Browns Flat	Greenwich	Morna	Simonds	**B**
Carter's Point	Greenwich Hill	Morrisdale	Smithtown	
Central Greenwich	Grove Hill	Mosher Hill	South Bay	
Centreton	Haggertys Cove	Moss Glen	Spruce Lake	
Chance Harbour	Hammond River	Musquash	Summerville	
Chapel Grove	Hampton	Nauwigewauk	Sunset Valley	
Chester	Hanford Brook	Nerepis	Titusville	
Clifton Royal	Hardings Point	New River Beach	Torryburn	
Coldbrook	Hardingville	Oak Point	Uphan	
Crystal Beach	Hillandale	Ononette	Victoria Beach	
Days Corner	Holderville	Orange Hill	Welch Cove	
Days Landing	Hunter Lake	Pamdence	Wells	
Dipper Harbour	Indiantown	Partridge Island	Westfield	
Drury Cove	Ingleside Heights	Perry Point	Whitehead	
Duck Cove	Ingleside	Petersville	Whites Bluff	
Eastmount	Johnson Croft	Pocolagan	Whites Mills	
Elmhurst	Keatings Corner	Primrose	Woodmans Point	
Epworth Park	Kennebecasis Park	Prince of Wales		

Saskatoon, Saskatchewan and surrounding area, including:

Allan	Dalmeny	Hawker	Rheinland	
Asquith	Delisle	Hawoods	Schoenweise	
Blucher	Dundurn	Hochstadt	Shields	
Blumenheim	Dunfermline	Indi	Strehlow	
Bradwell	Edzell	Langham	Thode	
Chappell	Elstow	Martensville	Vade	**B**
Cheviot	Farley	Meacham	Vanscoy	
Clavet	Floral	Neuhorst	Warman	
Colonsay	Furdale	Newcross	Whitecap	
Corman Park	Grandora	Osler	White Cap Reserve	
Cory	Grasswood	Pike Lake		

Census Metropolitan Area				Category
St. Catharines–Niagara Falls, Ontario and surrounding area, including:				
Allanburg	Fenwick	Pelham	Stevensville	
Beamsville	Fonthill	Port Colborne	Thorold	
Bertie	Fort Erie	Port Dalhousie	Vineland	
Bethel	Gasline	Port Robinson	Virgil	
Black Creek	Hanmer	Port Weller	Wainfleet	B
Black Horse Corner	Jordan	Queenston	Waverly Beach	
Chippawa	Jordan Station	Ridgemont	Welland	
Cooks Mills	Lincoln	Ridgeway	Winger	
Crescent Park	Merritton	Sherkston		
Crowland	Netherby	St. Davids		
Crystal Beach	Niagara-on-the-Lake	Stamford		
St. John's, Newfoundland and surrounding area, including:				
Bauline	Glenvilla Court	Middle Cove	Shea Heights	
Bay Bulls	Goulds	Mount Pearl	Shoe Cove	
Big Pond	Hogan's Pond	Outercove	St. Phillip's	
Blackhead	Irishtown	Paradise	St. Thomas	
Cahill Point	Kelligrews	Petty Harbour	Topsail	B
Conception Bay S.	Kilbride	Pleasantville	Torbay	
Donovans	Lance Cove	Portugal Cove	Upper Guilles	
Evergreen Village	Logy Bay	Pouch Cove	Wedgewood Park	
Flatrock	Maddox Cove	Quidi Vidi	Windsor Heights	
Foxtrap	Manuels	Seal Cove	Witless Bay	
Sudbury, Ontario and surrounding area, including:				
Azilda	Creighton	Levack	Skead	
Blezard Valley	Dowling	Lively	Stinson	
Cambrian Heights	Fairbank	Lockerby	Val Caron	
Capreol	Falconbridge	Milate	Val Therese	B
Chelmsford	Fingal	Naughton	Wahnapitae	
Coniston	Garson	Northern Heights	Whitefish	
Copper Cliff	Gatchell	Onaping	Worthington	
Thunder Bay, Ontario and surrounding area, including:				
Dorion	Murillo	Vickers Heights		B
Joynt	Pass Lake			
Toronto, Ontario and surrounding area, including:				
Acton	East Gwillimbury	Malvern	Preston Lake	
Agincourt	East York	Maple	Quantztown	
Ajax	Etobicoke	Markham	Queensville	
Alliston	Fairbank	Meadowvale	Rexdale	
Alton	Georgetown	Milliken	Richmond Hill	
Ansnorveldt	Glasgow	Milton	Roches Point	
Aurora	Goodwood	Mississauga	Rouge Hill	
Baldwin	Gormley	Moffat	Sayers Mills	
Belfountain	Greenwood	Mount Albert	Scarborough	
Black Creek Village	Holland Landing	Newmarket	Schomberg	
Bolton	Hornby	Nobleton	Sharon	
Bondhead	Huttonville	North Park	Sherwood	
Bramlea	Inglewood	North York	Snelgrove	A
Brampton	Islington	Norval	Springbrook	
Caledon Village	Jacksons Point	Oak Ridges	Stouffville	
Caledon	Keswick	Oakville	Streetsville	
Campbellville	Kettleby	Oakwood	Sutton West	
Cedar Valley	Kilbride	Old Mill	Tecumseth	
Cherrywood	Kings	Orangeville	Terra Cotta	
Claremont	Kleinburg	Palermo	Thornhill	
Concord	Lambton Mills	Palgrave	Tottenham	
Cooksville	Limehouse	Patterson	Udora	
Coventry	Liverpool	Pefferlaw	Unionville	
Deckers Hill	Locust Hill	Pickering	Uxbridge	
Downsview	Lowville	Port Credit	(continued)	

Census Metropolitan Area				Category

Toronto, Ontario and surrounding area, including: (continued)

				Category
Vaughan	Whitchurch	Woodbridge		A
West Hill	Whitevale	York		
Weston	Willowdale	Zephyr		

Vancouver, British Columbia and surrounding area, including:

				Category
Albion	Fraser Mills	Musqueam	Sea Island	
Aldergrove	Glen Valley	New Westminster	Shaughnessy	
Anmore	Hazelmere	Newton	Surrey	
Belcarra	Hollyburn	North Vancouver	Tsawwassen	
Bowen Island	Hopington	Ocean Park	Tynehead	
Brighton Beach	Horseshoe Bay	Pitt Meadows	Websters Corners	
Burnaby	Ioco	Port Coquitlam	West Vancouver	A
Cloverdale	Ladner	Port Hammond	Whalley	
Coquitlam	Langley	Port Kells	White Rock	
Delta	Lions Bay	Port Moody	Whonock	
Dollarton	Maillardville	Queensborough		
Dundarave	Maple Ridge	Richmond		
Fisherman's Cove	Matsqui	Roberts Bank		
Fort Langley	Mission	Sapperton		

Victoria, British Columbia and surrounding area, including:

				Category
Becher Bay	Cordova Bay	Langford	Rudlin Bay	
Brentwood Bay	Deep Cove	Luxton	Saanich	
Canoe Bay	Discovery Island	Metchosin	Saanichton	B
Central Saanich	Esquimalt	Millstream	Sidney	
Cole Bay	Goldstream	Oak Bay	Sooke	
Colwood	Hagan Bight	Patricia Bay	View Royal	

Windsor, Ontario and surrounding area, including:

				Category
Emeryville	Maidstone	Pike Creek	Tecumseh	B
Essex	McGregor	Rochester	Walkerville	
La Salle	North Woodslee	St. Joachim		

Winnipeg, Manitoba and surrounding area, including:

				Category
Anola	Gordon	Middlechurch	Ross	
Beach Junction	Grande Pointe	Monominto	Rosser	
Bergen	Gross Isle	Murray Park	Sapton	
Birds Hill	Hazelridge	Navin	Springfield	
Brokenhead	Headingley	Nourse	St. Clements	
Brooklands	Iles des Chenes	Oakbank	St. Francois Xavier	
Carman Junction	Kings Park	Ostenfeld	St. Germain	
Cartier	Kirkfield Park	Pigeon Lake	Ste. Agathe	A
Cooks Creek	Landmark	Pine Ridge	Ste. Genevieve	
Deacon	Less Crossing	Prairie Grove	Vermette	
Diamond	Linden	Queens Valley	Westwin	
Dufresne	Lorette	Richland	Whittier	
Dugald	Manlius	Ritchot		
Emesville	Meadows	Roblin		
Glass	Meadowvale	Roseland		
Glenlea	Melrose	Rosewood		

Appendix F
Low Income Cut-Off Table

(Effective until February 1, 2001)

Size of Family Unit	Size of Area of Residence				
	A	**B**	**C**	**D**	**E**
	500,000 and over	100,000-499,999	30,000-99,999	** Less than 30,000	Rural Areas
1 person	$17,571	$15,070	$14,965	$13,924	$12,142
2 persons	$21,962	$18,837	$18,706	$17,405	$15,178
3 persons	$27,315	$23,429	$23,264	$21,647	$18,877
4 persons	$33,063	$28,359	$28,162	$26,205	$22,849
5 persons	$36,958	$31,701	$31,481	$29,293	$25,542
6 persons	$40,855	$35,043	$34,798	$32,379	$28,235
7 persons	$44,751	$38,385	$38,117	$35,467	$30,928
For Each Additional Person	$3,896	$3,342	$3,319	$3,088	$2,693

** Includes cities with a population between 15,000 and 30,000 and small urban areas (under 15,000).

Attention Residents Of Québec

The *Ministère des Relations avec les citoyens et de l'Immigration* of the Québec government (MRCI) has income standards that differ from those of Immigration Canada. Please refer to Appendix B.

Citizenship and
Immigration Canada

Citoyenneté et
Immigration Canada

PROTECTED WHEN COMPLETED - **A**
PAGE 1 OF 4

APPLICATION TO SPONSOR
A MEMBER OF THE FAMILY CLASS AND UNDERTAKING (REGS. **April, 1997**)
REFER TO INSTRUCTIONS FOR HELP IN COMPLETING THIS FORM

FOR OFFICE USE ONLY		
Sponsor ID number ▶	CPC – CIC file number ▶	Kit identifier number ▶

Please print or type

A - SPONSOR

Fee receipt number ▶

1 Surname (Family name)	Surname before marriage	Given name(s)	2 Sex
			☐ Male ☐ Female

3 Date of birth	4 Country of birth	5 Marital Status (except for never married, please provide proof of marital status)
Day Month Year		☐ Never married ☐ Married ☐ Common-law ☐ Separated ☐ Divorced ☐ Widowed ☐ Annulled marriage

6 My home address is

No. & street   Apt./Unit

7 Mailing address   All correspondence should be mailed to box 6 ☐ or to:

No. & street   Apt./Unit

City/Town   Province   Postal code

City/Town   Province   Postal code

8 Home telephone no. Area code No.	9 Business telephone no. Area code No.	10 Facsimile no. Area code No.	11 Indicate most convenient time to reach you by telephone	Time ____ ☐ AM ____ ☐ PM

12 Canadian citizen ☐ Yes ☐ No	13 Permanent resident ☐ Yes ☐ No	14 Date of landing in Canada Day Month Year

15 This section applies to both permanent residents and naturalized Canadian citizens. Indicate country where immigrant Visa/ Record of Landing was processed.

Country ▶

Name (Surname and given name(s)) at time of landing

Record of landing number

16 Visa office preference (optional)

B - CO-SIGNER (Must be spouse or common-law spouse of sponsor)

FOR OFFICE USE ONLY
Co-signer ID number ▶

17 Surname (Family name)	Surname before marriage	Given name(s)

18 Sex ☐ Male ☐ Female	19 Date of birth Day Month Year	20 Country of birth	21 Relationship to sponsor ☐ Married to sponsor (Box 1) ☐ Common-law spouse of sponsor (Box 1)

22 Home telephone no. Area code No.	23 Business telephone no. Area code No.	24 Facsimile no. Area code No.	25 Indicate most convenient time to reach you by telephone	Time ____ ☐ AM ____ ☐ PM

26 Canadian citizen ☐ Yes ☐ No	27 Permanent resident ☐ Yes ☐ No	28 Date of landing in Canada Day Month Year

29 This section applies to both permanent residents and naturalized Canadian citizens. Indicate country where immigrant Visa/ Record of Landing was processed.

Country ▶

Name (Surname and given name(s)) at time of landing

Record of Landing number

IMM 1344A (01-2000) E

(DISPONIBLE EN FRANÇAIS - IMM 1344A F)

Canada

C - FAMILY MEMBERS BEING SPONSORED AND THEIR DEPENDENTS
(Print names in PINYIN if relatives live in the People's Republic of China)

30 Surname (Family name) (Include Surname before marriage) — Given name(s)	31 Relationship to sponsor	32 Date of birth D M Y	33 Country of birth	34 Marital status	35 Sex M | F	36 Type of dependent child
a) Family member you are sponsoring/principal applicant						☐A
ID no. (Office use only)		D M Y			☐ ☐	☐B ☐C
b) Spouse of person in a)						
ID no. (Office use only)		D M Y			☐ ☐	NOT APPLICABLE
c) Accompanying dependent children of persons in a) and b)						
1.						☐A
ID no. (Office use only)		D M Y			☐ ☐	☐B ☐C
2.						☐A
ID no. (Office use only)		D M Y			☐ ☐	☐B ☐C
3.						☐A
ID no. (Office use only)		D M Y			☐ ☐	☐B ☐C
4.						☐A
ID no. (Office use only)		D M Y			☐ ☐	☐B ☐C
d) Non-accompanying dependents of persons in a) and b)						
1.						☐A
ID no. (Office use only)		D M Y			☐ ☐	☐B ☐C
2.						☐A
ID no. (Office use only)		D M Y			☐ ☐	☐B ☐C

37 Address where your relative lives

No. & street   Apt./Unit

City/Town   Province/State/Region

Country   Postal code   Home telephone no.
                                    Area code | No

38 Mailing address for your relative   OR ☐ Same as in box 37

No. & street   Apt./Unit

City/Town   Province/State/Region

Country   Postal code

D - ADOPTION CASE

1. Please check one of the following boxes:

   ☐ Child already adopted abroad. Adoption order issued on: ▶   Day   Month   Year

   ☐ Child to be adopted abroad

   ☐ Child to be adopted in Canada

2. Child's country of residence/source country for adoption: _____

E - SPONSORSHIP OF A FIANCÉ(E)

1. I am free to marry;

2. I will marry my fiancé(e) within 90 days and will send a copy of the marriage certificate to the Case Processing Centre in Mississauga within 180 days of the date he/she becomes a permanent resident; and

3. I understand that if I fail to meet these conditions, my fiancé(e) will be reported under the *Immigration Act* and may be asked to leave Canada.

F - ELIGIBILITY ASSESSMENT

PART 1: If you answer "NO" to any questions in Part "1" you are not eligible to sponsor (or co-sign if applicable). You should NOT submit your application.

		SPONSOR	CO-SIGNER
a)	Are you 19 years of age or older?	☐ YES ☐ NO	☐ YES ☐ NO
b)	Are you a Canadian citizen or permanent resident?	☐ YES ☐ NO	☐ YES ☐ NO
c)	Are you sponsoring a member of the family class?	☐ YES ☐ NO	NOT APPLICABLE
d)	Are you residing in Canada and in no other country? * If you answered "NO", but you are a Canadian citizen living exclusively abroad, refer to the instructions. You may still be eligible to sponsor. Complete declaration Section G.	☐ YES ☐ NO	☐ YES ☐ NO

PART 2: If you answer "YES" to any questions in Part "2" you are not eligible to sponsor (or co-sign if applicable). You should NOT submit your application.

a)	Are you bankrupt as defined in the *Bankruptcy and Insolvency Act*?	☐ YES ☐ NO	☐ YES ☐ NO
b)	Have family members you previously sponsored received social assistance/welfare during the validity of the undertaking?	☐ YES ☐ NO	☐ YES ☐ NO
c)	Did you co-sign an undertaking where the sponsored family members received social assistance/welfare during the validity of the undertaking?	☐ YES ☐ NO	☐ YES ☐ NO
d)	Are you late in making a required payment on an immigration loan and have not made arrangements to defer payments?	☐ YES ☐ NO	☐ YES ☐ NO
e)	Are you currently in a jail, prison, penitentiary or reformatory?	☐ YES ☐ NO	☐ YES ☐ NO

PART 3: For Permanent Residents Only. If you answer "YES" to any of these questions, refer to instructions for more information.

a)	Have you been ordered to leave Canada?	☐ YES ☐ NO	☐ YES ☐ NO
b)	Have you been charged with a criminal offence that may be punishable by more than six months imprisonment? If yes, what was the charge and the date and place of the charge?	☐ YES ☐ NO	☐ YES ☐ NO

Charge: _____

Date: | Day | Month | Year | Place: _____

c)	Are you in violation of the *Immigration Act*?	☐ YES ☐ NO	☐ YES ☐ NO

G - RESIDENCY DECLARATION FOR CANADIAN CITIZENS LIVING EXCLUSIVELY OUTSIDE OF CANADA

1. I intend to live in Canada immediately after my spouse and/or children become permanent residents.

2. Please check one of the following boxes:

☐ My family and I intend to live in Quebec.　　　☐ My family and I intend to reside in a province other than Quebec.

H - CONSENT

I give consent to Citizenship and Immigration Canada to release all information pertaining to this sponsorship application to the person or firm named below and request that all related correspondence be directed to this Canadian representative.

Designated canadian representative	Name of firm, agency, etc. (if applicable)
Address - number and street	

City/town	Province	Postal code	Area code No.

I - UNDERTAKING

APPLIES TO RESIDENTS OF ALL PROVINCES/TERRITORIES, EXCEPT QUEBEC:

- I promise the Minister of Citizenship and Immigration to provide for the essential needs of the sponsored relative and their dependents who accompany them to Canada, if they are not self-supporting. I will provide food, clothing, shelter, and other goods or services, including dental care, eye care, and other health needs not provided by public health care. The money, goods or services provided by the sponsor and co-signer must be sufficient for the sponsored people to live in Canada. I understand that these obligations may be met by the sponsor alone, the co-signer alone, or by both of them.

- I promise that the sponsored relatives will not need to apply for social assistance/welfare.

- I make these promises so that the family members listed on this undertaking can be admitted to Canada as permanent residents. I understand that the family members will be admitted solely on the basis of their relationship to the sponsor and that they **do not** need to have the financial means to become established in Canada.

- I understand that this undertaking is valid for 10 years. It begins on the date the sponsored family members become permanent residents of Canada. It continues for 10 years no matter what may change in my life. For example, if I am divorced, change jobs, become unemployed, and/or go back to school, I will still be responsible to the relatives I am sponsoring or for whom I am co-signing.

- If I fail to keep my promise and do not provide for the essential needs of the sponsored relatives or they receive social assistance/welfare while I am responsible for them, I will be in default. I understand that a sponsor and co-signer continues to be in default until the sponsor or co-signer has repaid in full the amount of the benefits received or repaid the debt to the satisfaction of the social assistance authorities.

- All social assistance/welfare paid to the sponsored relative or any dependents becomes a debt owed by the sponsor and the co-signer to the Minister. As a result, the Minister has a right to take legal action in a court of law against the sponsor, the co-signer or against both of them. The Minister may take other actions to recover the debt from the sponsor or co-signer. The Minister may also assign the debt to a provincial government and that provincial government may then take legal action to collect any amount paid to my relatives. If the Minister has assigned the undertaking to a province, the effect is the same as if the sponsor and co-signer had given the undertaking to a provincial official.

- The Minister may choose not to take legal action to recover money from a sponsor or co-signer who has defaulted in a situation of abuse or in other circumstances. The decision of the Minister not to act at a particular time does not cancel the debt. The Minister may recover the debt when circumstances have changed.

- There are consequences for future undertakings if a sponsor or co-signer default on any sponsorship undertaking. This holds true for both this Undertaking and any past Undertakings where the sponsor or co-signer have not satisfactorily paid back their debts. If this is the case, neither the sponsor nor co-signer is allowed to sponsor or co-sign another application to sponsor a family class relative.

J - DECLARATION

APPLIES TO RESIDENTS OF ALL PROVINCES/TERRITORIES, EXCEPT QUEBEC:

- I agree to the terms outlined in Section I, Undertaking

APPLIES TO RESIDENTS OF ALL PROVINCES/TERRITORIES, INCLUDING QUEBEC:

- I declare that the information given on this form and any attached documents is complete, correct and fully discloses everything concerning my eligibility to sponsor or co-sign.

- I understand that false or misleading statements may lead to the refusal of the application for landing of the relatives I am sponsoring (or for whom I am a co-signer.) I understand that giving false or misleading information may be grounds for my prosecution and my relatives' removal from Canada.

- I understand all the above statements, having asked for and obtained an explanation on every point that was not clear to me.

K - SIGNATURE(S)

City/town				Province			
	Day	Month	Year			Day	Month	Year
Sponsor's signature		Date		Sponsor's spouses signature (if co-signer)			Date

OFFICIAL USE ONLY

Income requirements ▶		SA's available for ____		SA's required for ____		☐ Met	☐ Not met	☐ R 6(3)
☐ Sponsor's intention to marry verified			☐ Agreement and undertaking signed			Length of undertaking (Except Quebec) ▶		Years 1 0
Cost recovery code ▶	Amount		Receipt no.		ROLF ▶ ☐ Paid ☐ Loan ☐ Deferred ☐ N/A	# of person	$	
Lock-in date at Canada Immigration	Day Month Year	Signature of Immigration Officer ▶				Date signed ▶	Day Month Year	
Remarks ▶ ☐ See attached		Visa office ▶						

IMM 1344A (01-2000) E

I+I Citizenship and   Citoyenneté et
Immigration Canada Immigration Canada

FINANCIAL EVALUATION

Refer to the instruction guide for help in completing this form.
If you need more space, photocopy this form before you begin and submit all pages with your undertaking.

1 | NAMES

a) Sponsor's family (last) name	Given name(s)
b) Co-signer's family (last) name	Given name(s)

2 | ARE YOU RECEIVING GOVERNMENT ASSISTANCE?

Are you receiving government assistance? ☐ Yes ☐ No   Is your co-signer receiving government assistance? ☐ Yes ☐ No

If you answered yes for either of the above questions, please provide a copy of your last statement.

3 | TOTAL NUMBER OF PEOPLE FOR WHOM YOU WILL BE FINANCIALLY RESPONSIBLE

Number of people

3A SIZE OF FAMILY (Do not count family members more than once.)

i) Yourself **1**

ii) Your spouse .... ☐

iii) Your dependent children (whether they live with you or not) Please specify below   ☐

Name	Date of birth Day Month Year	Name	Date of birth Day Month Year
1.		3.	
2.		4.	

iv) Family class relatives you are sponsoring on this application (from Section C, Box 30, (a), (b) and (c) on "Application to Sponsor" (IMM 1344A))   ☐

v) Family class relatives you are sponsoring on this application but who will not be applying to immigrate to Canada (Section C, Box 30, (d) as above)   ☐

vi) Family class relatives you have sponsored in the past where the sponsorship is still in effect. Please specify below.   ☐

Name	Date of birth Day Month Year	Name	Date of birth Day Month Year
1.		3.	
2.		4.	

vii) Family class relatives you have sponsored who have not yet received permanent residence. Please specify below.   ☐

Name	Date of birth Day Month Year	Name	Date of birth Day Month Year
1.		3.	
2.		4.	

viii) Family class relatives for whom you have been a co-signer, where the sponsorship is still in effect. Please specify below.   ☐

Name	Date of birth Day Month Year	Name	Date of birth Day Month Year
1.		3.	
2.		4.	

IF YOUR SPOUSE IS A CO-SIGNER ON THIS SPONSORSHIP APPLICATION ADD:

ix) Family class relatives he/she has sponsored in the past where the sponsorship is still in effect. Please specify below.   ☐

Name	Date of birth Day Month Year	Name	Date of birth Day Month Year
1.		3.	
2.		4.	

x) Family class relatives he/she has sponsored who have not yet received permanent residence. Please specify below.   ☐

Name	Date of birth Day Month Year	Name	Date of birth Day Month Year
1.		3.	
2.		4.	

xi) Family class relatives for whom he/she has been a co-signer on an undertaking, where the sponsorship is still in effect. Please specify below.   ☐

Name	Date of birth Day Month Year	Name	Date of birth Day Month Year
1.		3.	
2.		4.	

3B FINANCIAL REQUIREMENT FROM LOW INCOME CUT-OFF TABLE

3 A) Total size of family unit (Add (i) to (xi)) ▶ ☐

3 B) Low Income Cut-off amount required ▶ $

(Enter this amount in Box 11)

4 YOUR EMPLOYMENT

The **qualifying period** * is the 12 months prior to the date your undertaking is received at this office. **You must attach proof of income.**

LIST ALL INCOME FOR WHICH YOU HAVE RECEIVED OR WILL RECEIVE A T-4

Employer's name, address & phone number	Name of supervisor	Occupation	Hours worked per week & rate per hour	Dates of employment From (Day Month Year)	To (Day Month Year)	Income during qualifying period *
a)						$
b)						$
c)						$

LIST ALL INCOME FROM SELF-EMPLOYMENT (BUSINESS AND PROFESSIONAL), IF ANY.
(You must attach proof, i.e., Statement of Income and Expense, Statement of Business Activities, etc.) $

Name of business (if applicable)	Percentage of share in business	Occupation/ position in company	Period of self-employment From (Day Month Year)	To (Day Month Year)	
					$
					$

TOTAL 4: TOTAL EMPLOYMENT INCOME FOR QUALIFYING PERIOD ▶ $

5 SPOUSE'S EMPLOYMENT INCOME (include only if your spouse has agreed to be a co-signer)

LIST ALL INCOME FOR WHICH YOUR SPOUSE HAS RECEIVED OR WILL RECEIVE A T-4

Employer's name, address & phone number	Name of supervisor	Occupation	Hours worked per week & rate per hour	Dates of employment From (Day Month Year)	To (Day Month Year)	Income during qualifying period *
a)						$
b)						$
c)						$

LIST ALL INCOME FROM SELF-EMPLOYMENT (BUSINESS AND PROFESSIONAL), IF ANY.
(You must attach proof, i.e., Statement of Income and Expense, Statement of Business Activities, etc.) $

Name of business (if applicable)	Percentage of share in business	Occupation/ position in company	Period of self-employment From (Day Month Year)	To (Day Month Year)	
					$
					$

TOTAL 5: TOTAL EMPLOYMENT INCOME FOR QUALIFYING PERIOD ▶ $

6

TOTAL "YOUR TOTAL INCOME" PLUS TOTAL "YOUR SPOUSE'S INCOME", IF YOUR SPOUSE IS CO-SIGNING ▶

6. Total Employment Income
$

INSERT TOTAL EMPLOYMENT INCOME FROM BOX 6 ON PREVIOUS PAGE ▶

6.
$

7 **INCOME FROM OTHER SOURCES FOR THE PAST 12 MONTHS (You must provide proof of this income.)**

	YOU	YOUR SPOUSE (if co-signer)
Rental income	$	$
Investment and interest income	$	$
Maternity/parental/sickness benefits	$	$
Pension income	$	$
Other income (please specify)	$	$

7A. Your TOTAL		7B. Your spouse's TOTAL		7C. TOTAL OTHER INCOME
$	+	$	=	$

8.
$

8 **TOTAL INCOME FROM ALL SOURCES (add box 6 and box 7C)** . . . .

9 **FINANCIAL OBLIGATIONS**

	YOU	YOUR SPOUSE (if co-signer)
	Amount of Payment over the past 12 months	Amount of Payment over the past 12 months
Mortgages on principal residence (except first mortgage)	$	$
Rents and mortgages on non-principal residences	$	$
Property and school taxes	$	$
Personal loans and lines of credit	$	$
Student loans	$	$
Immigration loans	$	$
All other loans	$	$
Business expenses	$	$
Rental expenses	$	$
Investment expenses	$	$
Interest due on credit cards	$	$
Alimony payments	$	$
Court directed payments	$	$
Income tax payments on arrears	$	$
Insurance payments (car, house, life and others)	$	$
Other	$	$

9A. Your TOTAL		9B. Your spouse's TOTAL		9C. TOTAL OBLIGATIONS
$	+	$	=	$

10. NET INCOME AVAILABLE
$

10 **AMOUNT AVAILABLE TO THE SPONSOR (Subtract box 9C from box 8)** . . . .

11. AMOUNT REQUIRED
$

11 **LOW INCOME CUT-OFF REQUIRED (Amount reported in box 3B)** . . . . ✱

✱ **IMPORTANT NOTE:** THE AMOUNT IN BOX 10 MUST BE EQUAL OR GREATER THAN THE AMOUNT IN BOX 11.
REFER TO THE INSTRUCTIONS FOR MORE INFORMATION.

12 FINANCIAL STATEMENT -- DECLARATION

I declare that the information given on the form, and in any documents attached, is complete, correct and fully discloses all of my financial obligations.

I understand that any false statements or concealment of any material fact on this form may lead to a refusal of the application for landing of the person I am sponsoring (or co-signing). I also understand that even though the person I am sponsoring (or co-signing) and their dependents may be admitted to Canada as permanent residents any false information on this form may be grounds for my prosecution and for their removal.

	Day	Month	Year
Signature of sponsor | | Date | |

	Day	Month	Year
Signature of sponsor's spouse (if co-signer) | | Date | |

13 OFFICIAL USE ONLY

TOTAL GROSS INCOME (6)	—	TOTAL FINANCIAL OBLIGATIONS (7C)	=	AMOUNT AVAILABLE TO SPONSOR (8)	AMOUNT REQUIRED (low income cut-off figure)

Financial criteria

☐ Met

☐ Not met

☐ R6(3)

	Day	Month	Year
Signature of Immigration Officer | | Date | |

Information to be provided on the Financial Evaluation form is collected under the authority of the *Immigration Act*. It is required for the purpose of determining your financial ability to provide for your relative(s) seeking admission to Canada. It may be used to enforce the undertaking you have signed, and it may be provided to provincial authorities pursuant to federal/provincial information exchange agreements. Information you provide on this form will be stored in personal information bank EIC PPU 240 and is protected and accessible under the provisions of the *Privacy Act* and the *Access to Information Act*. Instructions for obtaining information are provided in InfoSource, a copy of which is located in all Citizenship and Immigration offices.

■+■ Citizenship and   Citoyenneté et
     Immigration Canada   Immigration Canada

SPONSORSHIP AGREEMENT

This agreement is designed to help the sponsor, the co-signer (if applicable) and the sponsor's family class relative understand the obligations and responsibilities involved in sponsorships.

PARTIES

	NAME	DATE OF BIRTH		
		Day	Month	Year
Sponsor				
Co-signer (if applicable)				
Sponsored relative				

MUTUAL OBLIGATIONS

Canadian citizens and permanent residents are permitted to have their family class relatives join them in Canada only after signing a sponsorship undertaking. By signing the sponsorship undertaking, the sponsor and, if applicable, the co-signer promise:

☑ to provide for the sponsored relative and his/her dependent's essential needs for 10 years from the date the relatives receive permanent resident status;

Essential needs are food, clothing, shelter and other basic requirements for everyday living. It includes dental care, eye care and other health needs not covered by public health services

☑ that financial obligations or other personal circumstances over those 10 years will not prevent them from honouring the sponsorship commitment;

☑ that the sponsored relative and his/her dependents will not need to apply for social assistance/welfare benefits; and

☑ to respond promptly when asked for help by the sponsored relative and his/her dependents by giving money, buying items or providing services for living expenses.

If the sponsored relative and his/her dependents become permanent residents, they promise:

☑ to make every effort to provide for their own essential needs; and

☑ to ask their sponsors for help if they are having difficulty supporting themselves or meeting their own essential needs.

Canadä

IMPORTANT INFORMATION

Parents or grandparents who are sponsored are not expected to look for a job to care for themselves.

Sponsored relatives who are being abused or assaulted by their sponsors should seek safety away from their sponsors even if this means that they will have to apply for social assistance/welfare benefits. People in this situation will continue to be permanent residents and will be able to live in Canada. In this circumstance, sponsors will continue to be responsible for their relatives' essential needs for 10 years from the date the sponsored relatives were granted permanent residence.

LEGAL CONSEQUENCES

If the sponsor and, if applicable, the co-signer do not provide support as required, the sponsored relative can take legal action. In some cases, the Minister may assign the debt to a provincial government and that government may take legal action.

DECLARATION

I understand the contents of this agreement, having asked for and obtained an explanation on every point that was not clear to me.

Day	Month	Year

_____
Signature of sponsor   Date

Day	Month	Year

_____
Signature of co-signer (if applicable)   Date

Day	Month	Year

_____
Signature of sponsored relative   Date

▮✦▮ Citizenship and   Citoyenneté et
     Immigration Canada   Immigration Canada

STATUTORY DECLARATION OF COMMON-LAW UNION (REGS. April, 1997)

(IF APPLICABLE)

Canada PROVINCE OF	In the Matter of an Application to Sponsor a Member of the Family Class Pursuant to the *Immigration Act and Regulations* and In the Matter of Common-law Union
To Wit.	

We, (name of sponsor)   and, (name of co-signer)

of the (City, Town, Village)   of   county of   in the province of

Solemnly declare, that we have cohabited in a conjugal relationship for ___ continuous year(s) from [Day Month Year] to [Day Month Year]

---

1 My common-law spouse and I:

a) Have jointly signed a residential lease, mortgage or purchase agreement relating to a residence in which we both live. ☐ Yes ☐ No	b) Jointly own property other than our residence. ☐ Yes ☐ No	c) Have joint bank, trust, credit union or charge card accounts. ☐ Yes ☐ No	d) Have declared our common-law union under the *Income Tax Act* (T-1 "General - Individual Income Tax Return") ☐ Yes ☐ No

2 I have life insurance on myself which names my common-law spouse as beneficiary. ☐ Yes ☐ No

3 My common-law spouse has life insurance on him/herself which names me as beneficiary. ☐ Yes ☐ No

4 If none of the above sections applies what other documentary evidence do you have that would indicate your relationship as common-law spouses?

---

5 **SOLEMN DECLARATION**

We make this solemn declaration conscientiously believing it to be true, and knowing that it is of the same force and effect as if made under oath.

Name of Declarant (Sponsor)	Signature of Declarant (Sponsor)
Name of Declarant (Co-signer)	Signature of Declarant (Co-signer)
Declared before me at the (City, Town, Village)	Commissioner of Oaths (Name)
of county of	Signature of Commissioner of Oaths
in the province of	
this day of of the year	

IMM 5409 (02-1998) E   (DISPONIBLE EN FRANÇAIS - IMM 5409 F)   **Canadä**

 Citizenship and
Immigration Canada
Citoyenneté et
Immigration Canada

DOCUMENT CHECKLIST - SPONSOR

I have enclosed the following items in the envelope:

Put an "X" in the box when you have enclosed the item.
If you do not enclose all the required documents, your entire application will be returned to you.

FORMS

- Fees receipt stamped by financial institution (Do not send cash or personal cheques.) ☐
- Completed **Application to Sponsor a Member of the Family Class and Undertaking** (IMM 1344A) ☐
- Photocopy of the completed **Sponsorship Agreement** (IMM 1344B) signed by sponsor, co-signer and
  the sponsored relative (Except residents of Quebec) ☐
- Completed **Financial Evaluation** (IMM 1283) (Except residents of Quebec) ☐
- Completed **Document Checklist** (IMM 5287) ☐

PROOF OF PERMANENT RESIDENCE STATUS OR CANADIAN CITIZENSHIP

Photocopy of **ONE** of the following items:
- Record of Landing (IMM 1000) ☐
- Canadian birth certificate ☐
- Both sides of your Canadian Citizenship Card ☐
- Both sides of your Certificate of Registration of Birth Abroad ☐

IF YOUR SPOUSE WILL BE A CO-SIGNER

- Photocopy of your marriage certificate ☐
- Statutory Declaration of Common-law Union (if applicable) ☐
- Photocopy of **ONE** of the following items:
  - Spouse's Record of Landing (IMM 1000) ☐
  - Spouse's Canadian birth certificate ☐
  - Both sides of your spouse's Canadian Citizenship Card ☐
  - Both sides of your spouse's Certificate of Registration of Birth Abroad ☐

PROOF OF RELATIONSHIP TO THE SPONSORED FAMILY MEMBERS

- If you are sponsoring your **spouse**:
  - Marriage certificate ☐
- If you have had **previous marriages**:
  - Proof of legal separation (Income Tax Forms, legal documents) ☐
  - Divorce certificate ☐
  - Annulment certificate ☐
  - Death certificate for deceased spouse ☐
- If you are sponsoring your **parents**:
  - Birth certificate ☐
- If you are sponsoring an **adopted child**:
  - Adoption Order ☐

PROOF OF INCOME FOR SPONSOR AND, IF APPLICABLE, CO-SIGNER (Except Residents of Quebec)

For sponsor and, if applicable, co-signer, attach the following:
- An original computer printout of most recent Notice of Assessment and a computer printout of ALL income slips
  (e.g. T4, T4E, T5, T5007). These printouts may be obtained free-of-charge from Revenue Canada ☐

If applicable, also attach the following documents:
- If you or your co-signer are **employed**, also include:
  - Original letter from employer for the past 12 months stating salary, regular hours per week, and length of time employed; ☐
  - Photocopies of pay stubs for the last 12 months not covered by the Notice of Assessment and income slip printouts; and, ☐
  - Photocopy of your most recent T1 - Individual Income Tax Return ☐

PROOF OF INCOME FOR SPONSOR AND, IF APPLICABLE, CO-SIGNER (Except Residents of Quebec) (Continued)

- If you or your co-signer **received social assistance/welfare** in the last 12 months that is not listed on the computer printout of the T5007, also include:
  - Photocopy of receipt from welfare ☐
  - Photocopy of receipt from any other government payment ☐

- If you or your co-signer **received interest income** in the last 12 months that is not listed on the Notice of Assessment, also include:
  - Bank statement showing rate of interest, deposit amount, and length of time deposit held ☐

- If you and/or your co-signer are the **sole owners of a business, partners in a business,** and/or **corporate shareholders,** also include:
  - Photocopy of your most recent T1 - Individual Income Tax Return ☐
  - A "statement of business activities" from your accountant to cover January of the current year to the date of mailing of the sponsorship application ☐

- If you have other income in the last 12 months that is not listed on the Notice of Assessment, also include proof of:
  - Investment or Interest Income ☐
  - Rental Income (e.g. Statement of Real Estate Rentals) ☐
  - Pension Income ☐
  - Other(specify) ☐

FINANCIAL OBLIGATIONS FOR SPONSOR AND, IF APPLICABLE, CO-SIGNER

For financial obligations, attach proof of the following:

- All mortgages on principal residence (except first mortgage) ☐
- All rents and mortgages on non-principal residence ☐
- Property and school taxes ☐
- Personal loans and lines of credit ☐
- Student loans ☐
- Transportation loans from Citizenship and Immigration Canada ☐
- Right of Landing fee loan ☐
- All other loans ☐
- Business expenses (deductible under the Income Tax Act) ☐
- Investment expenses ☐
- Credit card interest (paid or due) ☐
- Alimony payments ☐
- Court directed payments (except child support) ☐
- Income tax payments on arrears ☐
- Insurance payments (car, house, life and others) ☐
- Other (specify) ☐

Have you addressed the envelope with the correct address and postage?
See "General Instructions" section for more information.

COMMON ERRORS WHICH DELAY PROCESSING

Incomplete applications will be returned. To avoid processing delays, you must enclose all the required items listed above. The most common reasons for returned applications are:

1. **Application to Sponsor a Member of the Family Class and Undertaking** form (IMM 1344A) is not signed.
2. The **Sponsorship Agreement** (IMM 1344B) has not been signed by the sponsor, co-signer (if applicable) and the sponsored family member.
3. All documents related to proof of income are not attached.
4. Financial Obligations section of the **Financial Evaluation** (IMM 1283) form is not complete.
5. Most recent Notice of Assessment and computer printouts of all income slips (T4, T4E, T5007) available from Revenue Canada are not attached.
6. Unless specifically requested, do NOT enclose income information that does not fall within the 12 months immediately preceding the mailing of your application, as it cannot be considered towards your income.

Undertaking of Assistance Form

This is the form that must be filled out by your relative. Your relative must complete the form as accurately as possible following the detailed instructions. The form also contains a Declaration and a Warning. Acting as sponsor, your relative has certain obligations to you, and this section of the form sets out those responsibilities. These responsibilities include the following: that your relative undertakes to provide for your room and board and general welfare, for a certain specified period, which is usually five or ten years.

This does not mean that you have to live with your relative or take money from your relative. It simply means that, during this specified period, should you become unable to support yourself financially, your sponsor is required to provide for you.

Your relative must sign this form and if your relative is married, his or her spouse should also sign the Undertaking.

Financial Evaluation Form

This is the other form your relative will have to fill out. Its purpose is to determine if your relative has the financial resources necessary to undertake responsibility for you and your dependants accompanying you to Canada.

Your relative needs to complete this form very carefully following the detailed instructions provided. Your relative has to calculate the size of the Family Unit (question 4 on the form, including you and your family) to determine if he or she has the financial resources to support you in Canada, should this be necessary.

Take a look at the 'Low Income Cut-Off of Family Units' provided in the kit. Let's assume you are married with one child. You will see that if your single relative is sponsoring you, resides in a large city, and has never sponsored anyone before, he has to be responsible for four (4) people – himself, you, your wife and your child – and will need to have a total annual income of at least Can\$30,655 to have his Undertaking approved.

While the family income level required of your relative is relatively modest, it increases quickly depending on the size of his or her family and the number of relatives for whom an Undertaking has been previously submitted.

DOCUMENTATION REQUIRED

Firstly, your relative has to include a copy of his or her **Immigrant Visa and Record of Landing** and/or **Canadian Citizenship** card for himself/herself and spouse.

Your sponsor also must provide documents to substantiate the funds he or she has indicated on the Financial Evaluation Form, such as bank records, savings account book, certificates of deposit, and so on. Banks in Canada routinely issue letters certifying the amount their clients have on account in the bank, and your relative should approach his bank for such a letter.

Your relative should also provide a letter from his or her employer, which must show the nature of his or her employment, present salary, the length of time employed there, and whether income and other taxes are deducted. If your relative is married, then a similar letter from his or her spouse's employer is also necessary.

Another essential point is that your relative must be able to provide some form of documentation indicating his relationship to you. For example, in the case of a spouse, a marriage certificate is essential. If your brother is in Canada, he should include a copy of his birth certificate and your birth certificate in order to prove the relationship.

Proving a relationship is often a very difficult matter. In some countries a birth certificate is not obtained by parents and may not be registered during the course of one's life. If your relative cannot prove the relationship and if your case is refused on these grounds, or for any reason whatsoever, your relative has a right to appeal to the Immigration Appeal Board in Canada. Note that even though you are the applicant and your relative in Canada is only assisting you, it is your relative who has a right to appeal and not you.

YOUR INTERVIEW AT THE CANADIAN IMMIGRATION OFFICE

As was pointed out in the overview of the process you will have to follow, you will normally be called for an interview with a Canadian immigration officer. This will take place after the Canadian High Commission, Embassy or Consulate has received instructions from Canada that your relative's Undertaking of

Assistance has been accepted and after you have submitted an Application for Permanent Residence in Canada.

The documentation required at your interview varies from office to office. You will normally receive a letter listing the specific documents required by the Canadian High Commission, Embassy or Consulate dealing with your application.

You should take along your passport and other travel documents. If you are married, you should take your marriage certificate. You should also take along proof of your assets, such as bank books and statements, certificates of deposit, and so on.

If you have any degrees or other educational certificates, diplomas, trade certificates, or professional membership letters, you should take the originals to the interview with you.

At the interview you will be asked some questions by the immigration officer. The most common of these are the following:

- Do you intend to work in Canada?

- Who are your relatives in Canada?

- How does the relationship come about?

- Why do you want to live in Canada?

- Have you visited Canada before? If so, where did you go? How long did you stay? What was the purpose of your trip? What were your impressions of Canada?

- How much money will you take with you to Canada? How much will you transfer later?

The above questions are only meant as guidelines for you to prepare for the interview. Keep in mind that as a Sponsored Dependant your educational and occupational qualifications are not taken into account. Basically, all you have to do is prove your relationship to your sponsor. But, you need to answer all the questions put to you, which may or may not include any or all of the above questions.

Answer each question as truthfully and completely as possible. There is a special section in Chapter 7, dealing exclusively with interviews for independent applicants. Some of it is relevant to you, too, so you might wish to read through it.

The next few chapters deal with Independent Applicants, and not Sponsored Dependants. If you are applying as a Sponsored Dependant, please skip to Chapter 6 entitled 'The Application Forms and Documents' and read through that chapter and subsequent chapters.

3

Independent Applicants

The process for an Independent Applicant to immigrate to Canada is much more involved than the one for a Sponsored Dependant.

DOCUMENTATION

Your first step is to consider all the documents you may need. The documents you will need might include the following, if applicable:

- your birth certificate

- your passport

- your marriage certificate

- your children's and spouse's birth certificates

- your divorce certificate or death certificate of your spouse

- police certificates of No Criminal Record

- military records

- passport size photographs of yourself and spouse and your dependants accompanying you

- evidence of your relationship to any relative in Canada

- your relative's Canadian passport, citizenship card, or Immigration Record and Visa

- any offers of employment in Canada you might have, or detailed business plans for Self-Employed Persons and Entrepreneurs

- evidence of investment in an Investor Fund in Canada

- records of all your assets, including your bank books, certificates of deposit as well as tax returns

- records of your past employment, including letters from your previous employers stating dates of employment, nature of work, etc.

- all your degrees, diplomas, trade certificates, professional membership cards

- any other supporting documents about yourself and your spouse that will be required by Canada Immigration or any other documents that you feel would support your application for permanent residence.

OVERVIEW OF THE PROCESS

After you have considered all the documentation that may be required, you should visit or write to the nearest Canadian immigration office and indicate your desire to receive an **Application for Permanent Residence**.

Interview

You should fill out the Application for Permanent Residence as carefully as possible and submit it along with the necessary documentation. If the application is accepted, you will be called for an interview with a Canadian immigration officer.

You will recall that there are 4 subsections within the Independent Applicant category:

1. Skilled Workers (intending to seek employment in Canada)

2. Entrepreneurs

3. Investors

4. Self-Employed Persons

Depending on your circumstances, and depending on the category in which you have applied, your application will be processed in different ways. These will be outlined later.

There are several possible outcomes to the interview. The immigration officer may refuse to consider your application further and find you not qualified to proceed to Canada. Or, he may approve it for you to go to Canada for employment.

Or, he may process your plans to establish or purchase a business in Canada under the Entrepreneur or Self-Employed categories. If your application is approved, the next step for all applicants is to undergo a medical examination and security check.

If you pass the medical and security checks, you will be issued a visa called an **Immigrant Visa and Record of Landing** and may proceed to Canada. After a check at the port of entry, and the completion of certain formalities, you will enter Canada as a permanent resident (landed immigrant).

All this may sound very confusing. However, we will take each step of the process and explain it in much greater detail.

Before doing this and advising you on how to maximise your chances of success in each situation, it is necessary to first evaluate your qualifications.

There is no point in going through the demanding exercise of applying for permanent residence in Canada and paying the substantial Government of Canada processing fee, if you are clearly not qualified.

PROCESSING AND RIGHT OF LANDING FEES

The current processing fee is Can$500 (Can$1,000 for business applicants), **plus** Can$500 for your spouse, **plus** Can$500 for each dependent child over 19 years of age, **plus** Can$100 for each child under 19 years of age. Additionally, a Right of Landing fee of Can$975 has been imposed for the applicant, his or her spouse and dependent children over 19 years of age. There is no fee for children under the age of 19.

The Processing Fee is non-refundable. However, the Right of Landing fee is refunded if an application is refused. You are not required to pay the Right of Landing fee until your application is provisionally approved.

THE POINT SYSTEM – AN OVERVIEW

Up to this point we have only discussed your options and narrowed down the best option for you. We have not examined your situation to see whether or not you have a realistic chance of being successful in your application. The process used to assess the hundreds of thousands of applications received every year is called the **Point System**.

The point system applies to every independent applicant. The norms of assessment do not change by the country of your citizenship, country of your application, officer doing the assessment, or any other special circumstance or situation. The norms of assessment are listed in Figure 2, simplified into non-technical language.

THE POINT SYSTEM IN DETAIL

We will now go through each of the factors listed in Figure 2 to help you evaluate your qualifications. Working charts follow to help you calculate your points.

1. Education
You can be awarded a **maximum of 16 units** for education as follows:

(a) **No units** if secondary (high) school has not been completed.
(b) **Five (5)** units if secondary school has been completed but the Diploma does not provide entrance to university.
(c) **Ten (10)** units if secondary school has been completed and the programme provides entry to university.
(d) **Ten (10)** units if secondary school has been completed and the completed programme includes trade or occupational certification.
(e) **Thirteen (13)** units if you have completed a post-secondary programme (of at least 1 year) admission to which requires secondary schooling at the level required for entry to univerisity.
(f) **Fifteen (15)** units if you have completed a Bachelor's degree.
(g) **Sixteen (16)** units if you have completed a Master's degree or Ph.D. degree.

2. Education and Training
The points awarded on Education and Training (ETF) are calculated according to the amount of formal professional and other training required for the particular occupation in which you are qualified, and intend to seek in Canada. The Canadian Government has established a code number for each job or occupation and publishes the code numbers in the *National Occupation Classification (NOC)*. Those code numbers are then converted into points for immigration purposes. Unfortunately, unless you live in Canada, it is very unlikely you will find these books in your local library.

Since there are several volumes of the *NOC* with some 30,000 job titles listed, it would be impossible to reproduce them all in

Factors	Assessment Criteria	Maximum Points
1. Education	Points are awarded for the years of secondary and post-secondary education you have successfully completed.	16
2. Education and Training	The award is measured by the amount of formal professional, vocational, apprenticeship, in-plant or on-the-job training necessary for average performance in the applicant's intended occupation.	18
3. Experience	Points are awarded for the years of experience you have in your occupation or in the business you plan to establish.	8
4. Occupational Demand	Points are awarded on the basis of the demand for the occupation in which you are qualified.	10
5. Arranged Employment	Points will be awarded to you if you have arranged employment in Canada, provided you have official approval for the job.	10
6. Levels Control (Demographic Factor)	From zero (0) to ten (10) points depending on predetermined immigration levels.	10
7. Age	If you are between 21 and 44 years old, you will be awarded the maximum points. Two points are subtracted for each full year you are over 44 or under 21.	10

Fig. 2   Assessment under the Point System.

8. Knowledge of French and English	If you are fluent in English and French, the two official languages of Canada, you will receive the maximum points. If you are fluent in one of the two languages you will receive nine (9) points.	15
9. Personal Suitability		10
Total		107
Pass Mark		70

Relatives in Canada
A bonus of five (5) points will be awarded to applicants with eligible relatives in Canada. An eligible relative has to be over 19 years of age and closer than a cousin.

this book. Chapter 4 provides more detailed information about the NOC.

3. Experience
The number of points you receive for the Experience factor depends on the years of experience you have in your occupation (see Figure 3).

• **Regardless of all other factors and considerations, unless you get at least two (2) points on this factor, your application will NOT be approved. In other words, you must have at least one year of experience in your intended occupation.**

4. Occupational Demand
The Occupational Demand factor is essential and usually makes the difference between acceptance or rejection. All applicants,

	Years of Experience			
ETF	1	2	3	4
1–2	2	2	2	2
5–7	2	2	4	4
15	2	4	6	6
17–18	2	4	6	8

Fig. 3. Experience assessment chart.

except Entrepreneurs, Self-Employed persons and Investors, must receive at least one (1) point on this factor before their application for permanent residence can be approved. If your occupation is not in demand and you receive no points on this factor, your application will almost certainly be refused.

Between zero (0) and ten (10) points are awarded, depending on the demand for workers in any particular occupation, as decided by the Immigration Department.

At the end of this chapter you will find a listing of all occupations currently having some demand and open to independent applicants (Figure 7).

- **Unless you intend to be an Entrepreneur, an Investor, or Self-Employed, you must get AT LEAST ONE POINT on this factor, in order for your application to be approved**.

5. Arranged Employment

You will get ten (10) points if you already have a job in Canada. But there is a catch. You must not only have a job waiting for you in Canada, but your employer must have *official sanction* to hire you, a non-resident of Canada, for the job.

You may think it will be rather easy for you to write to a friend or relative and arrange a job in Canada, or employ a third party such as an employment agency in Canada to find you a job. It is not that simple.

In order to obtain official approval to hire a non-resident for a job, a Canadian employer must approach the Canada Employment Centre nearest to the place of employment. The employer must then fill out a form called a Confirmation of Offer of Employment (EMP 5056).

The form requires detailed information about the name, address, and telephone number of the company, details about you, and about the job being offered to you. If the job title is one for which there are many Canadian residents available, the form will not be approved. If a job simply is described as a machine operator, for example, instead of a tool and die maker, although they might both be correct, the job offer may be refused because there are many general machine operators in Canada. The job description should be as detailed and specific as possible.

The employer must state the experience necessary for the job. The job offer must contain details of the related experience needed by anyone to meet the requirements, in addition to language or other skills that may be required.

The job must not be temporary, or only a temporary employment authorisation may be issued to you. The employer must state the fringe benefits and salary that will be paid to you, which, of course, must be above the minimum wage.

At this point you might be thinking that your friend or relative in Canada can make up a job offer that is so carefully matched to your situation that no one else can fulfil the requirements. That is not possible. The job has to be matched to your experience and qualifications.

The employer should take this form to the Canada Employment Centre (CEC), along with certain other documents. For example, the employer could advertise the job being offered in Canada, and then take along the advertisements and some proof that there are no persons in Canada suitably qualified for the job.

After the form has been accepted by the Canada Employment Centre, the form will not normally be approved immediately, although that can happen. First, the Canada Employment Centre will usually try to find a Canadian resident for the job. The job title, description and working conditions might be advertised and circulated to other Canada Employment Centres. Any person found available and qualified will be referred to the employer.

Your friend or relative cannot simply refuse to hire qualified people referred by the Canada Employment Centre, thereby keeping the job open to you. Approval to hire you will not be given in such a case, as officials will know there are qualified Canadian residents available for the job.

If there are no qualified Canadian residents found with the qualifications needed, the job offer may be approved, in which case the approval will be sent to the Canadian High Commission, Embassy or Consulate to which you have applied or will apply, and your application will be processed.

You should note that the process to obtain employment clearance can take weeks or months. Therefore, there are very few employers who will go through this rigorous procedure and wait for a long period of time to hire you, unless they have a very genuine need for your skills.

- **In short, it is not easy to obtain an approved offer of employment in Canada**.

6. Levels Control (Demographic Factor)

This factor (from 0 to 10 points) is regulated by Immigration to control the overall flow of immigrants. The points may be adjusted upwards or downwards to increase or decrease the number of applicants who would otherwise meet the selection criteria.

- **Eight (8) points are currently awarded to all applicants.**

7. Age

If you are between the ages of twenty-one (21) and forty-four (44), give yourself ten points. Deduct two points for every year you are over 44 or under 21.

8. Knowledge of Canada's Languages – English/French

If you are able to speak, read and write both English and French fluently, award yourself 15 points. (Fluently is defined as not needing language training after arrival in Canada.) If you are able to speak, read and write *either* English or French fluently, award yourself nine (9) points. If your ability is only to speak or to write or to read well either language, the points will be two (2) for each ability, and only one (1) if each ability is demonstrated with difficulty. In some countries (China in particular) you may have to have your language skills evaluated by an independent organisation.

9. Personal Suitability

Up to ten (10) points will be awarded by a Canadian immigration officer, based on his assessment of your prospects of becoming successfully established in Canada.

The assessment will be made by the officer at your interview. The number of points he awards you is totally at his discretion, although five (5) or six (6) out of 10 appears to be about average.

Ask yourself this question: given the Canadian way of life, how sure am I that I can successfully live there and integrate into society? Base your answer on your past experiences in moving, living in another country, on your knowledge of Canada, on your motivation, and so on. Now award yourself points between one and ten, based on your answer.

10. Relatives in Canada

Do you or your spouse have a relative in Canada, **closer** than a cousin, who is willing to help you? To be eligible your relative in Canada must be the mother, father, grandparent, brother, sister, uncle, aunt, nephew or niece of yourself *or* your spouse. If so, you may award yourself an extra five (5) points, provided you can prove the relationship.

We have now completed the point system. You should know that not all applicants have to meet all ten selection criteria.

A SELF-ASSESSMENT

You should now be ready to assess yourself.

Very carefully, you should go back to each factor and assess your points. Do *not* be generous with yourself or give yourself more points than you deserve. It is not in your interest to have anything but a realistic assessment.

You should also do an assessment of your spouse. Canadian law allows either spouse to apply for permanent residence. If your spouse were to apply and be approved, you and your unmarried children, if any, can accompany him or her to Canada. An assessment of your spouse will help you decide which of you should apply as the principal applicant.

SELF-ASSESSMENT CHARTS FOR EMPLOYMENT IN CANADA

Every independent applicant should fill in the table below. Even if you plan to be Self-Employed, an Investor or an Entrepreneur, do the points assessment for employment in Canada, which is based on nine (9) factors of the selection criteria (Figure 4).

If you have 70 or more points, there is a good chance of acceptance, and you should be called to interview. In some cases, the interview will be waived.

Now look at your grand total and that of your spouse. First, whose grand total is larger? If it is your spouse's then he or she should probably apply instead of you.

If you have between 65 and 70 points and either you or your spouse have an eligible relative in Canada, you still have a good chance.

Factor	Estimated Assessment of Yourself	Estimated Assessment of Your Spouse	Max.	Min Reqd.
1. Education	( )	( )	16	—
2. ETF	( )	( )	18	—
3. Experience	( )	( )	8	1
4. Occupational Demand	( )	( )	10	1
5. Arranged Employment	( )	( )	10	—
6. Levels Control	( )	( )	10	—
7. Age	( )	( )	10	—
8. Knowledge of English/French	( )	( )	15	—
9. Personal Suitability	(___)	(___)	10	=
TOTAL			107	70

Fig. 4. Self-assessment chart for employment in Canada.

- **Give yourself a bonus of five (5) points if either you *or* your spouse has a relative in Canada over 18 years of age who is closer than a cousin.**

If you have less than 70 points, and no eligible relatives in Canada, are you qualified to apply as an Entrepreneur or Investor, or a Self-Employed Person? If so, go to the tables below (Figures 5 and 6).

If you have less than 70 points and do not qualify in any of the above categories, then the chances of your application being accepted are not high. But there are always exceptions. For example, if you were educated in Canada and have returned to your home country and now have a year or two of occupational experience, the immigration officer might decide in your favour on a discretionary basis. Canadian immigration officers have the authority to recommend approval in situations where they consider the selection criteria do not accurately reflect your prospects of successful establishment in Canada. You may be able to take certain steps that could increase your qualifications so that you may re-apply at a later date. For example, if you did not receive the maximum points on the Education factor, you might consider going back to school or obtaining more training.

If you did not receive the maximum points on the Experience factor, you might wait a few years until you have more experience in your profession. Or, you might consider learning English or French or both, if you are not fluent in both languages.

As you should know by now, an approved job offer in Canada will dramatically increase the likelihood of your application being approved. So, you might attempt to obtain an approved offer.

The procedures discussed above might raise the number of points you will receive, should you decide to postpone your application or re-apply at some later date.

- **If you choose this route, remember to keep abreast of all changes in Canadian immigration procedures and policy, especially changes in the points awarded on the factors of Occupational Demand and Levels Control.**

Entrepreneur or Investor

If you have business experience and a substantial net worth (see Chapter 5) and are willing and able to transfer your assets to Canada, assess yourself in the table in Figure 5.

Now look at your grand total score. If it is over 25 points, a score which is relatively easy to obtain, then your application may be approved as an Entrepreneur or Investor.

If you have less than 25 points, but a successful background in

Factor	Estimated Assessment	Max.	Min Reqd.
1. Education	( )	16	—
2. ETF	( )	18	—
3. Experience	( )	8	1
4. Occupational Demand	Not Assessed	—	—
5. Arranged Employment	Not Assessed	—	—
6. Levels Control	( )	10	—
7. Age	( )	10	—
8. Knowledge of English/French	( )	15	—
9. Personal Suitability	(____)	10	=
TOTAL		107	25

Fig. 5. Self-assessment chart for Entrepreneur or Investor.

business, I recommend you go ahead and apply anyway. Canada is actively looking for Entrepreneurs and Investors and your application may still be approved at the discretion of the Immigration officer.

Self-Employed
If you have sufficient funds (see Chapter 5) to transfer to Canada and intend to be self-employed, you should assess yourself using the table in Figure 6.

Now look at your grand total score. If it is over 70 points, your application under the Self-Employed category may be approved.

SUMMARY

You have now assessed your chances of immigrating to Canada. If, after a realistic assessment, your prospects of immigrating to Canada look good, then proceed to the next few chapters dealing with separate stages of the process.

If your prospects do not look good in any category, then you might take some of the steps outlined earlier to improve your chances at some later date. If you cannot apply at this time, do not take it as a personal rejection of your qualifications. It merely

Factor	Estimated Assessment	Max.	Min Reqd.
1. Education	( )	16	—
2. ETF	( )	18	—
3. Experience	( )	8	1
4. Occupational Demand	Not Assessed	—	—
5. Arranged Employment	Not Assessed	—	—
6. Levels Control	( )	10	—
7. Age	( )	10	—
8. Knowledge of English/French	( )	15	—
9. Personal Suitability	(____)	10	=
TOTAL		107	25
Plus 30 if the officer believes you will become successfully established in your proposed business	+30		
GRAND TOTAL			

Fig. 6. Self-assessment chart for Self-Employed persons.

means that you cannot meet the requirements Canada has laid down. And remember, Canada receives hundreds of thousands of independent applications each year.

But, there is some good news. It seems clear that over the next few years increased immigration levels will be encouraged by the government. In addition, the Point System for selecting immigrants will certainly be revamped in the very near future.

While these changes are still at the discussion level, it seems the government wishes to amend the system to recruit flexible and adaptable people, rather than looking for specific skills or occupations that may not be in demand once an immigrant arrives in Canada.

A new system has been suggested by the Government which would emphasise post-secondary education and apprenticeship training, an ability to speak English and/or French and which for the first time would provide points for informal offers of employment in Canada.

It is proposed that there be no Occupational Demand List in the new system but significantly increase the points for skilled work experience.

Here is the proposed new point system:

Age	**Maximum 10**
– 21 to 44 years of age at time of application	10
– Lose 2 points for each year of age over 44 years or under 21 years	
Education	**Maximum 25**
– Doctorate and master's degrees	25
– Bachelor's degree involving equivalent of at least three years full-time studies	20
– Three-year equivalent full-time studies/training leading to a diploma, trade certificate or apprenticeship	20
– Two-year equivalent full-time studies/training leading to a diploma	15
– One-year equivalent full-time studies/training leading to a diploma	10
– High School	5
Language*	**Maximum 20**
– Fluency in first official language	16
– Reasonable abilities in first official language	8
– Poor or no abilities in first official language	0
– Fluency in second official language	4
– Reasonable abilities in second official language	0
– Poor or no abilities in second official language	0
*Points will be awarded on the basis of English and French abilities in four skills; speaking, reading, writing, and comprehension.	
Experience	**Maximum 25**
– One year of recent skilled work experience	10
– Two years of recent skilled work experience	15
– Three years of recent skilled work experience	20
– Four years of recent skilled work experience	25
Validated arranged employment	**Maximum 10**
– Arranged employment in Canada validated by HRDC	10
Adaptability	**Maximum 10**
– Spouse's (including common-law partner's) education Masters or PhD	5

Bachelor degree or three year diploma	4
One to two year post-secondary education	3
– Minimum one year full-time authorised work in Canada	5
– Minimum two year full-time post-secondary study in Canada	5
– Informal job offer in Canada in keeping with past experience of education	5
– Family member in Canada	5
Total	**Maximum 100**

Remember that the present Point System requires applicants to achieve a minimum 70 points out of a possible 107. The proposed new system has a maximum of 100 points, but the pass mark has not been established. Nevertheless, you might want to assess your points under the new system and, if you score 70 or more points, keep yourself fully informed about the new Point System.

If you are well educated, speak English and/or French and have good experience in a skilled occupation, even if it is not on the current Occupational Demand List, you may very well be able to comply with the new proposed selection criteria.

GENERAL OCCUPATIONS LIST

NOC*	Title	Occupational Factor	ETF**
A			
1111.2	Accountants	3	15
1431.0	Accounting and Related Clerks	1	5
2161.3	Actuaries	1	15
1441.0	Administrative Clerks	3	5
1221.0	Administrative Officers	1	7
1122.2	Advertising and Marketing Consultants	3	15
2255.3	Aerial Survey Technologists and Technicians	1	15
2146.0	Aerospace Engineers	5	17

Fig. 7.   General Occupations List.

NOC*	Title	Occupational Factor	ETF**
2148.1	Agricultural Engineers	5	17
2123.0	Agricultural Representatives, Consultants and Specialists	1	17
2272.1	Air Traffic Controllers	1	15
7437.0	Air Transport Ramp Attendants	1	5
2244.2	Aircraft Electrical Mechanics and Technicians	1	15
7315.2	Aircraft Inspectors	3	15
2244.1	Aircraft Instrument Mechanics and Technicians	1	15
7315.1	Aircraft Mechanics	1	15
6433.5	Airline Station Agents	1	7
2262.3	Airworthiness Inspectors	1	15
3213.0	Animal Health Technologists	5	15
5223.1	Animation Painters	1	2
5231.0	Announcers and Other Broadcasters	1	15
4169.1	Anthropologists	1	18
2211.2	Applied Chemical Technicians	1	15
2211.1	Applied Chemical Technologists	1	15
1235.3	Appraisers	1	7
2225.1	Arborists and Tree Service Technicians	1	15
4169.2	Archaeologists	1	18
2151.0	Architects	1	15
5113.0	Archivists	3	18
5131.4	Art Directors	3	15
2111.2	Astronomers	1	18
5225.0	Audio and Video Recording Technicians	5	7
3141.1	Audiologists	10	18
2244.4	Avionics Inspectors	1	15
2244.3	Avionics Mechanics and Technicians	1	15
B			
6252.0	Bakers	1	15
1434.1	Bank Clerks	1	5
6271.2	Barbers	1	2
2221.2	Biological Technicians	1	15

NOC*	Title	Occupational Factor	ETF**
2221.1	Biological Technologists	1	15
2121.1	Biologists	1	17
2148.2	Biomedical Engineers	5	17
7266.1	Blacksmiths	5	2
9491.1	Boat Assemblers	5	2
7262.0	Boilermakers	1	7
1231.0	Bookkeepers	1	7
5224.0	Broadcast Technicians	5	15
6463.2	By-Law Enforcement Officers	5	7
C			
7272.0	Cabinetmakers	1	7
7247.2	Cable Television Maintenance Technicians	3	7
7247.1	Cable Television Service Technicians	3	7
2255.1	Cartographic Technologists and Technicians	1	15
5244.1	Carvers	1	17
2231.2	Civil Engineering Technicians	1	15
2231.1	Civil Engineering Technologists	1	15
2131.0	Civil Engineers	5	17
3214.2	Clinical Perfusionists	10	15
7382.0	Commercial Divers	1	15
4212.0	Community and Social Service Workers	5	2
3131.1	Community Pharmacists and Hospital Pharmacists	1	17
2147.1	Computer Hardware Engineers	5	17
1421.0	Computer Operators	1	5
2163.0	Computer Programmers	10	15
2162.0	Computer Systems Analysts	10	15
1226.0	Conference and Event Planners	1	1
2224.0	Conservation and Fishery Officers	3	15
5212.1	Conservation and Restoration Technicians	1	7
5112.1	Conservators	3	15
2234.0	Construction Estimators	1	15

NOC*	Title	*Occupational* Factor	ETF**
7311.0	Construction Millwrights and Industrial Mechanics (except Textile)	10	7
7216.0	Contractors and Supervisors, Mechanic Trades	3	15
6242.0	Cooks	10	7
5223.2	Copy Stylists	1	2
5121.3	Copywriters	3	15
1244.1	Court Recorders	5	15
5244.8	Craft Instructors	1	15
5121.1	Creative Writers	3	1
0122.2	Credit Managers	3	15
5212.2	Curatorial Assistants	1	7
D			
3222.1	Dental Hygienists	5	15
3412.0	Dental Laboratory Bench Workers	1	2
3223.0	Dental Technicans	1	15
3221.0	Denturists	1	15
1423.1	Desktop Publishing Operator	3	7
7266.2	Die Setters	5	2
3132.0	Dietitians and Nutritionists	1	17
5131.2	Directors	3	15
5131.7	Directors of Photography	3	15
2253.2	Drafting Technicians	1	7
2253.1	Drafting Technologists	1	15
4216.2	Driver's Licence Examiners	1	1
4216.1	Driving Instructors	1	1
6681.1	Dry Cleaning and Laundry Machine Operators	1	2
E			
4163.0	Economic Development Officers and Marketing Researchers and Consultants	1	17
4162.0	Economists, Economic Policy Researchers and Analysts	1	17
1452.3	Editorial Assistants and Publication Clerks	3	5
5122.0	Editors	3	17

NOC*	Title	Occupational Factor	ETF**
4166.0	Education Policy and Researchers, Consultants and Program Officers	1	17
2241.2	Electrical and Electronics Engineering Technicians	1	15
2241.1	Electrical and Electronics Engineering Technologists	1	15
2133.0	Electrical and Electronics Engineers	5	17
7333.0	Electrical Mechanics	1	7
7244.0	Electrical Power Line and Cable Workers	5	15
3218.1	Electroencephalographic Technologists	10	15
3218.2	Electromyography Technologists	10	15
2242.0	Electronic Service Technicians (Household and Business Equipment)	1	7
6272.2	Embalmers	1	15
4213.0	Employment Counsellors	3	7
2148.3	Engineering Physicists and Engineering Scientists	5	17
1222.0	Executive Assistants	1	7
6241.1	Executive Chefs	10	7
5243.3	Exhibit Designers	1	15
F			
0721.0	Facility Operation Managers	1	15
4153.0	Family, Marriage and Other Related Counsellors	5	18
5243.2	Fashion Designers	1	15
5222.0	Film and Video Camera Operators	1	15
5131.5	Film Editors	3	15
5131.1	Film, Television and Radio Producers	3	15
1112.0	Financial and Investment Analysts	3	17
1111.1	Financial Auditors	3	15
1434.3	Financial Clerks	1	5
1114.2	Financial Examiners and Inspectors	3	7
1114.3	Financial Investigators	3	7
0111.0	Financial Managers	3	15
1114.1	Financial Planners	3	7

NOC*	Title	Occupational Factor	ETF**
6262.0	Firefighters	3	5
2222.1	Fish and Fish Products Inspectors	1	7
2272.2	Flight Dispatchers	1	15
2271.2	Flight Engineers (Second Officers)	1	15
5226.1	Floor Directors	1	15
2271.3	Flying Instructors	1	15
2148.4	Food Processing Engineers	5	17
2122.0	Forestry Professionals	1	17
2223.0	Forestry Technologists and Technicians	1	15
6272.1	Funeral Directors	1	15
7342.2	Furriers	1	2
G			
5226.3	Gaffers and Lighting Technicians	1	15
4169.3	Geographers	1	18
2255.5	Geographic Information System (GIS) Technologists and Technicians	1	15
2212.2	Geological and Mineral Technicians	1	15
2212.1	Geological and Mineral Technologists	1	15
2144.0	Geological Engineers	5	17
2113.0	Geologists, Geochemists and Geophysicists	1	17
5244.2	Glass Blowers	1	15
2225.2	Golf Course Superintendents	1	7
6243.0	Grain Elevator Operators	1	7
5241.0	Graphic Designers and Illustrating Artists	1	7
5227.1	Grips	1	7
7383.1	Gunsmiths	5	7
H			
6271.1	Hairstylists	1	2
7312.0	Heavy-Duty Equipment Mechanics	10	7
4169.4	Historians	1	18
4164.2	Home Economics	1	15
2225.3	Horticulturalists	1	15
4164.3	Housing Policy Analysts	1	15

NOC*	Title	Occupational Factor	ETF**
I			
6481.1	Image Consultants	1	5
4211.4	Independent Paralegals	1	7
2141.0	Industrial and Manufacturing Engineers	5	17
2252.0	Industrial Designers	1	15
7242.0	Industrial Electricians	5	15
2233.2	Industrial Engineering and Manufacturing Technicians	1	15
2233.1	Industrial Engineering and Manufacturing Technologists	1	15
2243.0	Industrial Instrument Technicians and Mechanics	5	15
3131.2	Industrial Pharmacists	1	17
2263.0	Inspectors in Public and Environmental Health and Occupational Health and Safety	5	7
2262.4	Inspectors, Weights and Measures	1	15
1233.1	Insurance Adjusters	3	7
1233.2	Insurance Claims Examiners	3	7
1434.2	Insurance Clerks	1	5
1234.0	Insurance Underwriters	3	7
5242.0	Interior Designers	1	15
4164.4	International Aid and Development Project Officers	1	15
5125.3	Interpreters	1	15
1114.4	Investment Underwriters	3	7
J			
7344.1	Jewellers and Related Workers	1	15
5123.0	Journalists	3	15
K			
5226.2	Key Grips	1	15
L			
2152.0	Landscape Architects	1	17

NOC*	Title	Occupational Factor	ETF**
2225.4	Landscape Designers, Landscape Architectural Technicians and Technologists	1	15
2225.5	Landscape Gardeners	1	7
2225.6	Landscapers	1	7
4211.1	Legal Assistants and Paralegals	1	15
1242.0	Legal Secretaries	5	15
5223.6	Lettering Artists	3	2
5111.0	Librarians	3	18
5211.0	Library and Archive Technicians and Assistants	1	15
4169.5	Linguists	1	18
1232.0	Loan Officers	3	5
7383.2	Locksmiths	5	7
M			
7316.0	Machine Fitters	1	7
9481.1	Machine Operators, Electrical Apparatus Manufacturing	1	2
7231.2	Machining and Tooling Inspectors	5	15
7231.1	Machinists	1	15
7332.2	Major Appliance Repairers/ Technicians	1	15
5226.5	Make-Up Artists	1	15
1122.1	Management Consultants	3	15
2148.5	Marine and Naval Engineers	5	17
2115.3	Materials Scientists	1	17
2161.1	Mathematicians	1	18
2232.2	Mechanical Engineering Technicians	1	15
2232.1	Mechanical Engineering Technologists	1	15
2132.0	Mechanical Engineers	5	17
7321.2	Mechanical Repairers, Motor Vehicle Manufacturing	1	7
3211.1	Medical Laboratory Technologists	5	15
1243.0	Medical Secretaries	5	7
3216.0	Medical Sonographers	5	15
1244.2	Medical Transcriptionists	5	15
5244.3	Metal Arts Workers	1	15

NOC*	Title	Occupational Factor	ETF**
2142.0	Metallurgical and Materials Engineers	5	17
2115.1	Metallurgists	1	17
2213.0	Meteorological Technicians	1	15
2114.0	Meteorologists	1	17
2121.2	Microbiologists, Cell and Molecular Biologists	1	17
7342.3	Milliners	1	2
2143.0	Mining Engineers	5	17
5227.2	Motion Picture Projectionists	1	7
7322.0	Motor Vehicle Body Repairers	1	2
7321.1	Motor Vehicle Mechanics and Technicians	1	7
2262.1	Motor Vehicles Defects Investigators	1	15
7334.0	Motorcycle and Other Related Mechanics	1	7
5212.4	Museum Extension Officers	1	7
5212.3	Museum Guides and Interpreters	1	7
5212.5	Musuem Registrars and Cataloguers	1	7
N			
2261.0	Nondestructive Testers and Inspectors	3	5
3215.2	Nuclear Medicine Technologists	5	15
O			
3143.0	Occupational Therapists	10	17
8615.0	Oil and Gas Drilling, Servicing and Related Labourers	1	2
3233.2	Operating Room Technicians	1	15
3414.1	Orthopaedic Technologists	1	7
3144.0	Other Professional Occupations in Therapy and Assessment	10	15
7445.0	Other Repairers and Servicers	1	2
7335.0	Other Small Engine and Equipment Mechanics	1	7
5226.7	Other Workers in Motion Pictures, Broadcasting and the Performing Arts	1	15

NOC*	Title	Occupational Factor	ETF**
P			
5223.3	Paste-Up Artists	1	2
4161.3	Patent Agents	1	15
3211.2	Pathologists' Assistants	5	15
5245.0	Patternmakers – Textile, Leather and Fur Products	1	7
1223.0	Personnel and Recruitment Officers	3	15
2145.0	Petroleum Engineers	5	17
2255.2	Photogrammetric Technologists and Technicians	5	15
5221.0	Photographers	1	2
2111.1	Physicists	1	18
3142.0	Physiotherapists	10	17
2271.1	Pilots	1	15
4169.6	Political Scientists	1	18
5244.4	Potters	1	15
7352.2	Power Station Operators	1	7
7243.0	Power Station Electricians	1	15
7352.1	Power Systems Operators	1	7
5212.6	Preparators	1	7
4155.1	Probation and Parole Officers	5	7
1473.0	Production Clerks	3	5
5124.0	Professional Occupations in Public Relations and Communications	1	15
5245.0	Program Leaders and Instructors in Recreation and Sport	5	5
1224.0	Property Administrators	1	5
5227.3	Props Person and Set Dressers	1	7
3219.3	Prosthetists and and Orthotists	10	15
4151.0	Psychologists	3	18
4169.7	Psychometricians	1	18
7422.0	Public Works Maintenance Equipment Operators	1	2
1225.0	Purchasing Agents and Officers	1	15
R			
3215.3	Radiation Therapists	10	15
3215.1	Radiography Technologists	5	15

NOC*	Title	Occupational Factor	ETF**
2262.2	Railway Accident Investigation Officers	1	15
7314.0	Railway Carmen/Women	1	2
7361.1	Railway Locomotive Engineers	1	7
2275.1	Railway Traffic Controllers	1	7
5131.6	Record Producers	3	15
7383.3	Recreational Vehicle Repairers	1	7
7313.0	Refrigeration and Air Conditioning Mechanics	1	7
2255.4	Remote Sensing Technologists and Technicians	5	15
7441.0	Residential and Commercial Installers and Servicers	1	2
3214.1	Respiratory Therapists	10	15
6233.0	Retail and Wholesale Buyers	1	15
6421.0	Retail Salespersons and Sales Clerks	3	2
S			
7383.4	Safe and Vault Servicers	5	7
6441.0	Sales Representatives, Wholesale Trade (Non-technical)	3	7
4143.0	School and Guidance Counsellors	1	17
5227.4	Script Assistants	1	7
7342.4	Seamstresses	1	2
1241.0	Secretaries (except Legal and Medical)	5	7
4216.3	Sewing Instructors	1	1
7261.0	Sheet Metal Workers	1	7
7343.2	Shoe Repairers	1	2
7374.1	Shoemakers	1	2
5223.4	Sign Painters	1	2
7332.1	Small Appliance Servicers and Repairers	1	7
4164.1	Social Policy Researchers	1	15
4164.5	Social Survey Researchers	1	15
4152.0	Social Workers	5	17
4169.8	Sociologists	1	18
2147.2	Software Engineers	5	17
2115.2	Soil Scientists	1	17

NOC*	Title	Occupational Factor	ETF**
6241.2	Sous-Chefs	10	7
1121.0	Specialists in Human Resources	3	15
3141.2	Speech-Language Pathologists	10	18
5224.5	Stained Glass Artists	1	15
7351.0	Stationary Engineers and Auxiliary Equipment Operators	5	7
2161.2	Statisticians	1	18
7252.1	Steamfitters and Pipefitters	1	7
1472.0	Storekeepers and Parts Clerks	3	2
5224.6	Stringed Instrument Makers	1	15
7263.0	Structural Metal, Platework Fabricators and Fitters	1	15
5226.4	Stunt Co-ordinators and Special Effects Technicians	1	15
7222.0	Supervisors, Motor Transport and other Ground Transit Operators	5	7
2254.2	Survey Technicians	1	15
7246.2	Switch Network Installers and Repairers	1	15
T			
7342.1	Tailors and Dressmakers	1	2
5212.8	Taxidermists	1	7
6221.0	Technical Sales Specialists, Wholesale Trade	1	15
5121.2	Technical Writers	3	17
7246.4	Telecommunications Equipment Technicians	1	15
7245.0	Telecommunications Line and Cable Workers	3	15
7246.3	Telecommunications Service Testers	1	15
7246.1	Telephone Installers and Repairers	1	15
5125.2	Terminologists	1	18
2148.6	Textile Engineers	5	17
7317.0	Textile Machinery Mechanics and Repairers	1	7
5243.1	Theatre Designers	1	15
7232.0	Tool and Die Makers	5	15

NOC*	Title	Occupational Factor	ETF**
4211.3	Trade Mark Agents	1	15
1113.2	Traders	3	7
5125.1	Translators	1	18
1476.0	Transportation Route and Crew Schedulers	3	5
6431.0	Travel Counsellors	1	15
1114.5	Trust Officers	3	7
U			
7341.0	Upholsterers	1	7
2153.0	Urban and Land Use Planners	1	17
V			
3114.0	Veterinarians	1	18
W			
5226.6	Wardrobe Supervisors	1	15
7344.2	Watch Repairers	1	7
7265.0	Welders	1	15
Y			
7361.2	Yard Locomotive Engineers	1	7

* NOC = National Occupational Classification
** ETF = Educational and Training Factor

4

National Occupation Classification (NOC) and Occupational Demand

NATIONAL OCCUPATION CLASSIFICATION (NOC)

The National Occupation Classification (NOC) points are determined by the government of Canada for each of the over 30,000 job titles in NOC.

OCCUPATIONAL DEMAND

You should go through the list of occupational titles at the end of Chapter 3 to find the one best suited to you. You will see that this listing also lists the points for the Educational and Training Factor (ETF).

The individual job titles are not always perfectly clear. You really need access to the NOC to see the specific job descriptions, but since the NOC contains some 30,000 job descriptions, that is not possible in this book.

The list in Chapter 3 contains only those occupations which are currently 'in demand' and which receive some points on the factor of Occupational Demand. If your occupation is not on the list, you will almost certainly be refused, since your intended occupation must have at least one (1) point on the Occupational Demand factor in order to be approved. However, as noted in the Preface, the Immigration Department will probably move away from the Occupational Demand factor shortly.

In this chapter, we provide only a sample of Job Descriptions from the National Occupational Classification (NOC). You might be able to see the entire NOC at your local library – it's worth asking.

If your prospects do not look good in any occupation, then you might take some of the steps outlined earlier to improve your chances at some later date. If you cannot comply at this time, do not take it as a personal rejection of your qualifcations. It merely means that you cannot meet the requirements Canada has laid

	Education/Training	**Other**
SKILL LEVEL A	• University degree (bachelor's, master's or postgraduate)	
SKILL LEVEL B	• Two to three years of post-secondary education at community college, institute of technology or CEGEP *or*	• Occupations with supervisory responsibilities are assigned to skill level B.
	• Two to four years of apprenticeship training *or*	• Occupations with significant health and safety responsibilities
	• Three to four years of of secondary school and more than two years of on-the-job training, training courses or specific work experience.	(e.g. fire fighters, police officers and registered nursing assistants) are assigned to skill level B.
SKILL LEVEL C	• One to four years of secondary school education.	
	• Up to two years of on-the-job training, training courses or specific work experience.	
SKILL LEVEL D	• Up to two years of secondary school and short work demonstrations or on-the-job training.	

Fig. 8.   NOC Skill Level Criteria.

down which, quite frankly, do not always make very good sense. And remember, Canada receives hundreds of thousands of independent applications each year.

However, as noted in the Preface, the Occupational Demand list will probably be eliminated and replaced by the NOC Skill Level Criteria. This means that work experience in a skilled occupation at levels A and B will be favoured, without reference to any particular occupation.

1111 FINANCIAL AUDITORS AND ACCOUNTANTS

Financial auditors examine and analyse the accounting and financial records of individuals and establishments to ensure accuracy and compliance with accounting procedures. Accountants plan, organise and administer accounting systems for individuals and establishments. Articling students in accounting firms are included in this unit group. Financial Auditors and Accountants are employed by auditing and accounting firms throughout the private and public sectors or they may be self-employed.

Examples of titles classified in this unit group

Accountant
Chartered Accounts (C.A.)
Certified General Accountant
   (C.G.A.)

Certified Management
   Accountant (C.M.A.)
Financial Auditor
Internal Auditor

Main duties
Financial auditors perform some or all of the following duties:

- Examine and analyse journal and ledger entries, bank statements, inventories, expenditures, tax returns and other accounting and financial records, documents and systems of an individual, department, company or other establishment to ensure financial recording accuracy and compliance with established accounting standards, procedures and internal controls.

- Prepare detailed reports on audit findings and make recommendations to improve individual or establishment's accounting and management practices.

- Conduct field audits of businesses to ensure compliance with provisions of the Income Tax Act, Canadian Business Corporations Act or other statutory requirements.

- May supervise other auditors.

Accountants may perform some or all of the following duties:

- Plan, set up and administer accounting systems and prepare financial information for an individual, department, company or other establishment.
- Examine accounting records and prepare financial statements and reports.
- Develop and maintain cost finding, reporting and internal control procedures.
- Examine financial accounts and records and prepare income tax returns from accounting records.
- Analyse financial statements and reports and provide financial, business and tax advice.
- May act as a trustee in bankruptcy proceedings.
- May supervise articling students or other accountant.

Employment requirements

- Chartered accountants require a university degree
  and
  Completion of a training programme approved by the Institute of Chartered Accountants and several years of on-the-job training
  and
  Accreditation by the Institute of Chartered Accountants.

- Certified general accountants and certified management accountants require completion of secondary school and usually require some post-secondary education related to accounting
  and
  Completion of a training programme approved by the Society of Certified General Accountants or Society of Management Accountants and several years of on-the-job training
  and
  Accreditation by the Certified General Accountants Association or the Society of Management Accountants.

- Auditors require education, training and accreditation as indicated for chartered accountants, certified general accountants or certified management accountants
  and
  Some experience as an accountant.

- Auditors may require accreditation by the Institute of Internal Auditors.

- To act as a trustee in bankruptcy proceedings, auditors and accountants must hold a licence as a trustee in bankruptcy.

2131 CIVIL ENGINEERS

Civil Engineers plan, design, develop and manage projects for the construction or repair of various structures such as buildings, roads, airports, railways, rapid transit facilities, bridges, dams, ports and coastal installations and systems related to highway and transportation services, water distribution and sanitation. Civil Engineers may also specialise in foundation analysis, building and structural inspection, surveying and municipal planning. Civil Engineers are employed by engineering consulting companies, municipal and other levels of government, and in many other industries, or they may be self-employed.

Examples of titles classified in this unit group

Bridge Engineer	Public Works Engineer
Civil Engineer	Sanitation Engineer
Construction Engineer	Structural Engineer
Environmental Engineer	Surveying Engineer
Highway Engineer	Traffic Engineer
Hydraulic Engineer	Transporation Engineer
Municipal Engineer	Water Management Engineer
Project Engineer, Construction	

Main duties

Civil Engineers perform some or all of the following duties:

- Confer with clients and other members of the engineering team and conduct research to determine project requirements.

- Plan and design major civil projects such as buildings, roads, bridges, dams, water and waste management systems and structural steel fabrications.

- Develop construction specifications and procedures.

- Evaluate and recommend appropriate building and construction materials.

- Interpret, review and approve survey and civil design work.

- Conduct field services for civil works.

- Ensure construction plans meet guidelines and specifications of building codes and other regulations.

- Establish and monitor construction work schedules.

- Conduct feasibility studies, economic analyses, municipal and regional traffic studies, environmental impact studies or other investigations.

- Conduct technical analyses of survey and field data for development of topographic, soil, hydrological or other information and prepare reports.

- Act as project or site supervisor for land survey or construction work.

- Prepare contract documents and review and evaluate tenders for construction projects.

- Supervise technicians, technologists and other engineers and review and approve designs, calculations and cost estimates.

Employment requirements

- A bachelor's degree in civil engineering or in an appropriate related engineering discipline is required.

- Registration as a Professional Engineer (P.Eng.) by a provincial or territorial association of professional engineers is often required for employment and to practise as a civil engineer.

- Engineers are eligible for registration following graduation from an accredited educational programme and after at least two years of supervised work experience in engineering and, in some provinces, after passing a professional practice examination.

- In some provinces, those who are not graduates of an accredited educational programme are eligible for registration after completing a six to eight-year term of supervised employment and successfully passing examinations.

- In Quebec, membership in the professional corporation for engineers is mandatory.

- Supervisory and senior positions in this unit group require experience.

2163 COMPUTER PROGRAMMERS

Computer programmers write computer programs by coding sets of instructions into machine-readable form. They are employed in computer software and consulting firms and in programming units throughout the private and public sectors.

Examples of titles classified in this unit group

Application Programmer	Programmer Analyst
Business Programmer	Scientific Programmer
Computer Programmer	Software Development
Operating Systems	Programmer
Programmer	Software Programmer
Programmer – Computer Systems	Systems Programmer

Main duties

Computer Programmers perform some or all of the following duties:

- Write computer programs or software packages by coding instructions and algorithms into machine-readable form.

- Test, debug, document and implement computer programs or software packages.

- Maintain existing computer programs by making minor modifications as required.

- Act as a resource person, solving computer problems for users.

Employment requirements

- A bachelor's degree in computer science or in another discipline with a significant programming component, such as mathematics, commerce or business administration
  or
  Completion of a college programme in computer science is usually required.

- Specialisation in commercial or engineering and scientific applications requires specific post-secondary study or experience.

- Senior positions in this unit group, such as programmer analyst, require experience.

Additional information

- Progression to computer systems analyst is possible with experience.

Classified elsewhere

- *Computer Operators* (1421)

- *Computer Systems Analysts* (2162)

- Computer service technicians (in 2242 *Electronic Service Technicians [Household and Business Equipment]*)

- Computer training representatives (in 4131 *College and Other Vocational Instructors*)

3215 MEDICAL RADIATION TECHNOLOGISTS

This unit group includes technologists who operate radiographic and radiation therapy equipment to administer radiation treatment and produce images of body structures for the diagnosis and treatment of injury and disease. They are employed in hospitals, cancer treatment centres, clinics and radiological laboratories. Medical radiation technologists who are supervisors or instructors are included in this unit group.

Examples of titles classified in this unit group

Clinical Instructor, Radiation
  Therapy
Mammography Technician
Nuclear Medicine Technologist
Radiation Therapist
Radiation Therapy Technologist

Radiography Technologist
Radiotherapy Technician
Supervisor, Nuclear
  Medicine Technologists
X-Ray Technician

Main duties
Radiography technologists perform some or all of the following
duties:

- Operate X-ray, radiographic and fluoroscopic equipment,
  specialised C.T. scanners and mammography units to produce
  radiographs or images of body structures for the diagnosis by
  radiologists of disease or injury.

- Record and process patient data.

- Perform scheduled maintenance and minor emergency repairs
  on radiographic equipment.

- May train and supervise student radiographers or supervise
  other radiography technologists.

Nuclear medicine technologists perform some or all of the following duties:

- Prepare radiopharmaceuticals, such as radionuclides and other
  materials and administer them to patients or to biological
  samples.

- Operate radiation detection equipment, such as gamma
  cameras, scanners, scintillation counters and ionisation
  chambers, to acquire data for use by nuclear medicine
  physicians in the diagnosis of disease.

- Perform diagnostic procedures using radioactive materials on
  biological specimens, such as blood, urine and faeces.

- Record and process results of procedures.

- Check equipment to ensure proper operation.

- May train and supervise student nuclear medicine technologists or supervise other nuclear medicine technologists.

Radiation therapists perform some or all of the following duties:

- Operate linear accelerators, cobalt 60, X-ray and other radiation therapy equipment to administer radiation treatment prescribed by radiation oncologists.

- Check radiation therapy equipment to ensure proper operation.

- Assist radiation oncologists and clinical physicists with preparation of radiation treatment plan.

- Assist in the preparation of sealed radioactive materials such as cobalt, radium, cesium and isotopes and the construction of devices such as plaster casts and acrylic moulds to assist with the administration of radiation treatment.

- May train and supervise student radiotherapy technologists or supervise other radiotherapy technologists.

Employment requirements

- Completion of a two to three-year college, hospital school or other approved programme in diagnostic radiography (for radiography technologists), nuclear medicine technology (for nuclear medicine technologists) or radiation therapy (for radiation therapists)
  and
  A period of supervised practical training are required.

- Medical radiation technologists require registration with the Canadian Association of Medical Radiation Technologists or a provincial counterpart or an appropriate provincial governing body.

- In Quebec, membership in the professional corporation for radiology technicians is mandatory.

4152 SOCIAL WORKERS

Social workers treat social functioning difficulties, provide counselling, therapy and referral to other supportive services, and evaluate child development and the adequacy of child care. They are employed by hospitals, school boards, social service agencies, welfare organisations and correctional facilities, and may also work in private practice.

Examples of titles classified in this unit group

Co-ordinator of Social Work
Medical Social Worker
Psychiatric Social Worker

Social Work Supervisor
Social Worker

Main duties
Social Workers perform some or all of the following duties:

- Interview clients individually, in families, or in groups, to assess their situation and problems and determine the types of services required.

- Provide counsel and therapy to assist clients in developing skills to deal with and resolve their social and personal problems.

- Plan programmes of assistance for clients including referral to agencies that provide financial assistance, legal aid, housing, medical treatment and other services.

- Investigate cases of child abuse or neglect and take authorised protective action when necessary.

- Serve as members on interdisciplinary teams of professionals working with client groups.

- Act as advocates for client groups in the community and lobby for solutions to problems directly affecting client groups.

- Develop or advise on social policy, conduct social research, and assist in community development.

- May supervise other social workers.

Employment requirements

- A bachelor's degree in social work is required.

- In Alberta, a master's degree in social work is required.

- Supervised practical experience is usually required.

- Successful completion of provincial written and/or oral examinations is usually required.

- A provincial certificate of registration is required by Newfoundland, Prince Edward Island, New Brunswick, Quebec and Saskatchewan.

- Membership in a provincial Association of Social Workers is usually required.

- In Quebec, membership in the professional corporation for social workers is mandatory.

Classified elsewhere

- *Community and Social Service Workers* (4212)

- *Family, Marriage and Other Related Counsellors* (4153)

- *Managers in Social, Community and Correctional Services* (0314)

- *School and Guidance Counsellors* (4143)

5111 LIBRARIANS

Librarians develop, organise and maintain library collections and provide advisory services for users. They are employed in libraries or in a department within a library.

Examples of titles classified in this unit group

Bibliographer	Library Consultant
Cataloguer	Supervisor, Library
Librarian	

Main duties
Librarians perform some or all of the following duties:

- Recommend acquisition of books, periodicals, audio-visual and other materials for inclusion in library collection.

- Classify and catalogue library materials.

- Prepare bibliographies, indexes, reading lists, guides and other finding aids.

- Develop systems to access library collections.

- Perform manual and online reference searches, make inter-library loans and perform other functions to assist users in accessing library materials.

- Provide specialised programmes such storytime reading for children.

- Conduct library information and orientation training sessions.

- Supervise library technicians, assistants and clerks.

Employment requirements

- A master's degree in library science is required.

Additional information

- Progression to library management positions is possible with experience.

Classified elsewhere

- Library managers (in 0511 *Library, Archive, Museum and Art Gallery Managers*)

- Medical records librarians (in 1413 *Records and File Clerks*)

- School librarians (in 4141 *Secondary School Teachers* and 4142 *Elementary School and Kindergarten Teachers*)

6241 CHEFS

This unit group includes various types of chefs who plan and direct food preparation and cooking activities and who prepare and cook meals and specialty foods. They are employed in restaurants, hotels, hospitals and other health care institutions, central food commissaries, clubs and similar establishments, and on ships.

Examples of titles classified in this unit group

Chef Head	Chef
Chef de cuisine	Master Chef

Chef de partie	Pastry Chef
Corporate Chef	Saucier
Executive Chef	Sous-chef
Executive Sous-chef	Specialist Chef
Garde Manger, Chef	

Main duties

Executive chefs perform some or all of the following duties:

- Plan and direct food preparation and cooking activities of several restaurants in an establishment, restaurant chains, hospitals, or other establishments with food services.

- Plan menus and ensure food meets quality standards.

- Estimate food requirements and may estimate food and labour costs.

- Supervise activities of sous-chefs, specialist chefs, chefs and cooks.

- Recruit and hire staff.

- May prepare and cook food on a regular basis, or for special guests or functions.

Sous-chefs perform some or all of the following duties:

- Supervise activities of specialist chefs, chefs, cooks and other kitchen workers.

- Demonstrate new cooking techniques and new equipment to cooking staff.

- May plan menus and requisition food and kitchen supplies.

- May prepare and cook meals or specialty foods.

Chefs and specialist chefs perform some or all of the following duties:

- Prepare and cook complete meals, banquets or specialty foods, such as pastries, sauces, soups, salads, vegetables and meat, poultry and fish dishes, and create decorative food displays.

- Instruct cooks in preparation, cooking, garnishing and presentation of food.
- Supervise cooks and other kitchen staff.
- May plan menus.
- May requisition food and kitchen supplies.

Employment requirements

- Completion of secondary school is usually required.
- Completion of a three-year cook's apprenticeship programme
  or
  Formal training abroad
  or
  Equivalent training and experience are required.
- Cook's trade certification is available in all provinces except Quebec, the Northwest Territories and the Yukon.
- Executive chefs usually require several years of experience in commercial food preparation, including two years in a supervisory capacity
  and
  Experience as a sous-chef, specialist chef or chef.
- Sous-chefs, specialist chefs and chefs usually require several years of experience in commercial food preparation.

Additional information

- There is some mobility among the various types of chefs in this unit group.
- Executive chefs may progress to managerial positions in food preparation establishments.

Classified elsewhere

- *Cooks* (6242)
- *Food Service Counter Attendants and Food Preparers* (6641)

7232 TOOL AND DIE MAKERS

Tool and Die Makers make, repair and modify custom-made, prototype or special tools, dies, jigs, fixtures and gauges which require precise dimensions. They are employed primarily in manufacturing industries and in tool and die, mould making and machine shops. Tool and die maker apprentices are included in this unit group. This unit group also includes patternmakers and metal mould makers.

Examples of titles classified in this unit group

Die Finisher
Die Maker
Jig Maker
Metal Mould Maker
Metal Patternmaker

Mould Maker – Plastics Processing
Tool and Die Maker
Tool and Die Maker Apprentice
Tool Maker

Main duties

Workers in this unit group perform some or all of the following duties:

- Read and interpret drawings and specifications of tools, dies, prototypes or models.

- Compute dimensions and tolerances and set up machine tools.

- Position, secure, measure and work metal stock or castings to lay out for machining.

- Operate a variety of machine tools to cut, turn, mill, plane, bore, grind or otherwise shape workpiece to prescribed dimensions and finish.

- Verify machined parts for conformance to specifications using precision measuring instruments.

- Fit and assemble parts using hand tools.

- Machine, fit and assemble casting and other parts to make metal patterns, core boxes and match plates.

- Machine, fit and assemble parts to make metal moulds for plastic injection moulding or other production processes.

- Inspect and test completed tools, dies, jigs or fixtures for proper operation.

Employment requirements

- Some secondary school education is required.

- Completion of a four-year tool and die making apprenticeship programme
  or
  A combination of over five years of work experience in the trade and some high school, college or industry courses in tool and die making is usually required to be eligible for trade certification.

- Tool and die making trade certification is available, but not compulsory, in Nova Scotia, Ontario, Manitoba and Alberta.

- Interprovincial trade certification (Red Seal) is also available to qualified tool and die makers.

- Mould makers may require completion of an apprenticeship or a college programme in mould making.

- Pattern makers may require completion of an apprenticeship or a college programme in patternmaking.

- Mould making and patternmaking trade certification is available, but not compulsory in Ontario.

Additional information

- Progression to supervisory positions is possible with experience.

- Red Seal trade certification allows for interprovincial mobility.

Classified elsewhere

- *Machinists and Machining and Tooling Inspectors* (7231)

- Supervisors of tool and die makers (in 7214 *Contractors and Supervisors, Metal Forming, Shaping and Erecting Trades*)

5

Entrepreneurs, Self-Employed Persons and Investors

Canada is actively seeking immigrants who will either establish or purchase a business interest in Canada. Such persons are called entrepreneurs. An entrepreneur is a person who organises, manages and assumes the risks of a business or enterprise.

In this chapter we will outline the business categories open to you as an entrepreneur, self-employed person or investor so that you can decide which option best suits your situation.

ENTREPRENEURS

Definition

For Canadian immigration purposes, an entrepreneur means a person who has the ability to establish, purchase or make a substantial investment in a business in Canada that will create or maintain jobs for Canadian residents. In addition, it means someone who will take an *active part* in the management of the business. A passive investment will not suffice.

The applicant in this category must show an ability to manage a business based on his or her past experience. This does not mean, necessarily, that the applicant have a background in business, although that generally is the case. For example, a school principal without previous business experience might be approved as an entrepreneur if he or she were purchasing an interest in a private school in Canada, where that applicant had knowledge of educational requirements and was to be involved in the management of the school.

Unconditional visa

There are two ways in which an entrepreneur may apply. Firstly, he or she may apply for an unconditional visa. This usually means that the applicant must invest in a business before arrival in Canada. The applicant needs to prove that a financial and legal commitment has already been made to establish, purchase or make an investment in a specified business in Canada. Usually the applicant will have visited Canada before applying for permanent residence and thoroughly researched a project. In practice however, very few Unconditional Visas are issued.

Conditional visa

The alternative is to apply for a conditional visa. This means that the applicant may receive an immigrant visa but it will contain a condition that the immigrant must establish a business within two years of arrival in Canada. In other words, within a two-year period, the immigrant must approach a Canada Immigration Centre in Canada and provide evidence of having invested and created employment opportunities in a business in which the immigrant is actively involved in the management.

Business proposals

In the past, a detailed business proposal was required of most entrepreneurs. This is no longer a mandatory requirement, although one may be requested by the Immigration authorities during the processing of applicants applying for an unconditional visa. Should you be required to file a detailed business proposal, you would be well advised to seek the assistance of a professional consultant. Unless you have a thorough knowledge of Canadian business procedures and are fully versed in the legal and financial aspects of setting up a business in Canada, it will be difficult for you to successfully write and present a business proposal to the Canadian Immigration authorities without someone in Canada to assist you.

Recommendation

If you are applying as an entrepreneur, you are recommended to apply for a conditional visa. This will eliminate the need for a detailed business proposal. You will only have to prove two things:

- First, that you have a successful business or managerial background, and sincerely intend to live and do business in Canada.

- Second, that you have sufficient funds to establish a business in Canada, and provide for your establishment.

No specific amount of money is laid down in the Canadian Immigration Regulations. As a rule of thumb, you would normally have to be in a position to transfer Can$250,000 and plan to invest at least Can$100,000 in a business in Canada. But there is no hard and fast rule: it depends very much on your business or managerial background and your ability to convince the immigration officer of your prospects of successfully establishing yourself in business in Canada.

On a practical business level, the advantage of applying for a conditional visa is that you give yourself time after arrival in Canada to establish contacts within the business community and familiarise yourself with Canadian business practices, before having to make a financial commitment.

Experience shows that immigrants who rush into a business enterprise before becoming familiar with business conditions often make serious investment mistakes and/or are taken advantage of by unscrupulous individuals, usually within their own ethnic community.

SELF-EMPLOYED

Definition

A self-employed person is an immigrant who has the ability and intends to establish a business in Canada that will create an employment opportunity for himself or herself and will make a significant contribution to the economic, cultural or artistic life of Canada.

Primarily, this refers to farmers, artists, sports personalities and to a lesser extent to the operators of small businesses which certain communities may need.

I find that very few persons are considered in this category. Most businesses, however small, will require at least one employee and the immigration authorities will usually consider even the smallest business enterprise as an entrepreneurial applicant.

However, the successful author, sports or artistic personality who can document personal success in his or her own country will usually be favourably considered in this category.

INVESTORS

Definition

An investor is an immigrant who has successfully operated, controlled or directed a financially successful business or commercial undertaking, and who has by his or her own endeavours accumulated a net worth of at least Can$800,000. An investor normally is not actively involved in the project. Usually, he or she is making a passive investment.

It is important to note that this definition of an investor varies in a subtle way from that of an entrepreneur. The definition of entrepreneur refers to the ability to operate a business in Canada. This does not necessarily mean that an entrepreneur must have previous business experience. An investor, however, must have practical business experience. But this does not mean that an investor has to have owned and operated his own business. A senior executive employee whose duties are key to the successful operation of a substantial business and who makes senior management decisions for a company would meet the criteria.

At the same time, the successful entrepreneur, perhaps someone owning and operating a very small retail outlet, would also meet the definition.

Professional persons

Immigration does not generally consider that self-employed professionals such as doctors, dentists, lawyers, accountants, architects and other professionals qualify under the Investor category. When the Investor programme was introduced, the policy was to accept professionals only if they had significant business experience. This policy seems to be changing and applicants who are professionals may now find it much easier to comply with the requirements as an investor.

At the present time, an investor is required to invest Can$400,000 for a period of five (5) years. However, there are financing arrangements that can be made with financial institutions where only Can$150,000 has to be paid up-front.

I would recommend that investors consult with a reputable consultant in Canada before making an investment.

Investors' options

The investment options open to investors were severely curtailed on 1 July 1996.

Prior to that date, privately administered venture capital funds were approved by the Federal Government in all provinces of Canada. However, all such private funds were allowed to expire on 30 June 1996 and no new private funds will be approved in the foreseeable future. The exception is the Province of Quebec which operates its own immigration investor programme.

This leaves only government administered funds open to investors.

Advantages of the Investor category

The primary attraction and advantage of the Investor category is that an unconditional visa is issued to the investor, and he or she need not worry about establishing and operating a business in Canada, nor about conditions removed. An investor is free to work, study, go into business, etc. without any further contact with the Immigration authorities. He or she can reside wherever they wish in Canada, irrespective of the Province in which they invest.

WHAT IS THE CANADA IMMIGRANT INVESTOR PROGRAMME?

The Immigrant Investor Programme allows you to gain permanent residence in Canada by making a five-year investment of Can$400,000 in the Canadian economy. Your investment is government guaranteed and will be repaid in full, without interest, at the end of that period.

The provinces and territories of Canada will use the capital to develop their economies and create jobs. These provinces/territories also offer many services to assist you in business life and in settling into Canada. *For specific information on these services, please contact the provincial/territorial governments listed at the end of this chapter (Figure 9).*

While the programme has existed since the 1980s, as of April 1, 1999, it has been completely updated and simplified. It is now a single national programme managed by Citizenship and Immigration Canada (CIC) on behalf of the provinces/territories. To enter, you must meet the requirements for qualification and follow the straightforward immigration process.

Who qualifies?

You have an excellent chance to qualify for the Programme if you have business experience, sufficient net worth and the funds to invest. In order to become an Immigrant Investor, you must meet the following requirements. You have:

- Successfully operated, controlled or directed a business.

- Accumulated a personal net worth of Can$800,000 through your own efforts.

- Paid Can$400,000 to the Receiver General for Canada prior to being issued a visa.

The Immigration Process

If you qualify as an Immigrant Investor you can take the following steps to enter the Immigrant Investor Programme. Please note that you must also meet the medical and security requirements.

1. Download an *Immigration Application – Business form* and the *Guide for Business Applicants* from the CIC website *http://www.cic.gc.ca*, or obtain copies from one of the Business Immigration Centres. Business Immigration Centres are visa offices that deal with all immigration matters and provide expertise in business immigration. The Centres are in Beijing, Bonn, Buffalo, Damascus, Hong Kong, London, Paris, Seoul and Singapore.

2. Submit your completed visa application form, together with all supporting documents, to one of the nine Business Immigration Centres. The Centres will advise you of any further documentation that may be required.

3. Once your application has been examined, you may be required to attend an interview.

4. Once all immigration matters have been addressed at the Business Immigration Centre, you must sign a Subscription Form and pay the Can$400,000 investment to CIC Headquarters in Ottawa before a visa will be issued.

5. You will receive your immigration visa.

What happens next?

Once you have settled in Canada as a permanent resident, you will enjoy all the same social benefits as Canadian citizens. Your family will have access to the excellent schools and health care in your community. Provincial and territorial governments can provide considerable expertise to help you with your business endeavours.

Travel outside Canada for business reasons is understood to be part of the business person's lifestyle. Short business trips will not affect your permanent resident status. You should check with a Canada Immigration Centre before leaving Canada to ensure that you will not lose your status.

As permanent residents, you and your dependants have the right to live, study and work indefinitely in Canada. You can apply for Canadian citizenship and a passport after fulfilling certain basic requirements. Further information is available from local citizenship offices in Canada.

Five good things about the Immigrant Investor Programme

1. Entering Canada's Immigrant Investor Programme is a single, simple process.

2. Your investment is government guaranteed. After five years, you get your full capital back.

3. You can choose to live anywhere in Canada.

4. Virtually every cultural and ethnic community exists within Canada. You need not feel like a stranger in your new land.

5. Canada is the largest trading partner of the United States and has excellent trade relationships in the Americas and around the world. Most Canadians speak English and many speak French, making Canada an ideal place to conduct a business, whether local or international.

Exploratory visits
It is a good idea to visit Canada before applying as a permanent resident. Depending on your country of origin, you may be required to obtain a Canadian visitor visa. When you visit Canada, you can explore its possibilities as a place of business and a great place to live.

On the Web
For more information on Business Immigration and the Immigrant Investor Programme, visit the Internet site at *http://www.cic.gc.ca*

The Charter of Rights and Freedom
The constitution of Canada contains a *Charter of Rights and Freedoms*, which sets out certain rights that are enjoyed by all residents. These include a wide range of legal rights as well as the freedom of speech, association and peaceful assembly.

Highly developed
For six years in a row in the 1990s, Canada was ranked no. 1 among 174 countries in the United Nations Human Development Index, which measures a country's well-being.

Success so far
Over 70,000 investors and their dependants have taken part since Canada's Immigrant Investor Programme began in 1986.

The Quebec Programme
Under the terms of the Canada-Quebec Accord, the Canadian province of Quebec can select business immigrants for its own Immigrant Investor Programme. The applications of investors choosing Quebec are processed in cooperation with the Government of Canada. Investors in Quebec must agree to reside in Quebec. Applicants will be selected by Quebec to qualify for an immigrant visa and must also meet federal immigration requirements.

PROVINCIAL GOVERNMENT CONTACTS FOR BUSINESS IMMIGRATION

Newfoundland
Trade and Investment Division Industry, Trade and Technology, P.O. Box 8700, St John's, Newfoundland A1B 4J6. Tel: (709) 729-2781. Fax: (709) 729-5936. Internet: *http://www.success.nfld.net*

Nova Scotia
Business Immigration, Nova Scotia Economic Development and Tourism Business Development Corporation, P.O. Box 519, 1800 Argyle Street, Suite 601, Halifax, Nova Scotia B3J 2R7. Tel: (902) 424-6864. Fax: (902) 424-6823. Internet: *http://www.novascotiabusiness.com*

New Brunswick
New Brunswick Department of Economic Development, Tourism and Culture, P.O. Box 6000, Fredericton, New Brunswick E3B 5HI, Tel: (506) 453-3981. Fax: (506) 444-4277. Internet: *http://www.gov.nb.ca/NBFirst*

Prince Edward Island
Immigration Investment and Trade Policy Division, Department of Development, 75 Fitzroy Street, 2nd Floor, Charlottetown, Prince Edward Island C1A 1R6. Tel: (902) 368-6252. Fax: (902) 368-5886. Internet: *http://www.gov.pe.ca*

Quebec
Ministère des Relations avec les Citoyens et de l'Immigration, Direction de L'Aide à L'Immigration d'Affaires, 360 McGill Street, Montréal (Québec) H2Y 3E9. Tel: (514) 864-9191. Téléc.: (514) 864-3825. Internet: *http://www.immq.gouv.qc.ca/daia*

Fig. 9.   Canada Immigrant Investor Programme.

Ontario
Business Immigration Section, Ministry of Economic Development and Trade, Hearst Block, 5th Floor, 900 Bay Street, Toronto, Ontario M7A 2E1. Tel: (416) 325-6986. Fax: (416) 325-6653. Internet: *http://www.2ontario.com/bi/home.html*

Manitoba
Department of Industry, Trade and Tourism, 410–155 Carleton Street, Winnipeg, Manitoba R3C 3H8. Tel: (204) 945-2466. Fax: (204) 957-1793. Internet: *http://www.gov.mb.ca/itt/trade*

Saskatchewan
Department of Economic and Cooperative Development, 5th Floor, Office Tower Delta Regina, 1919 Saskatchewan Drive, Regina, Saskatchewan S4P 3V7. Tel: (306) 787-9212. Fax: (306) 787-3872. Internet: *http://www.gov.sk.ca/econdev*

Alberta
Business Immigration Program, Alberta Economic Development, 5th Floor, Commerce Place, 10155-102 Street, Edmonton, Alberta T5J 4L6. Tel: (780) 427-6419. Fax: (780) 427-6560. Internet: *http://www.gov.ab.ca/edt/bip*

British Columbia
British Columbia Immigration Office, Ministry of Employment and Investment, 655-999 Canada Place, Vancouver, British Columbia V6C 3E1. Tel: (604) 844-1810. Fax: (604) 660-4092. Internet: *http://www.ei.gov.bc.ca/immigration*

Yukon
Industry, Trade and Investment Department of Economic Development, P.O. Box 2703, Suite 400, 211 Main Street, Whitehorse, Yukon Y1A 2C6. Tel: (867) 667-5466. Fax: (867) 667-8601. Internet: *http://www.economicdevelopment.gov.yk.ca*

Northwest Territories
Investment Development, Trade and Investment Division, Department of Resources, Wildlife and Economic Development, Government of the Northwest Territories, P.O. Box 1320, 3rd Floor, Northern United Place, Yellowknife, Northwest Territories X1A 2L9. Tel: (867) 920-8969. Fax: (867) 873-0101. Internet: *http://www.rwed.gov.nt.ca*

Nunavut
Department of Sustainable Development, Government of Nunavut, P.O. Box 1340, Iqaluit, Nunavut X0A 0H0. Tel: (867) 979-5070. Fax: (867) 979-5920. (Internet site not available)

6

The Application Forms and Documents

GATHERING INFORMATION

By now, you should have been able to decide on the best category in which to apply.

The next step in the immigration process is to gather all the necessary documents and information. You will need to provide some of these documents with the **Application for Permanent Residence**, and some for verification at the interview.

Documents generally required

The following are the documents *usually* needed. Note that this is not an exhaustive list, and that you may need other documents, depending on your particular situation and case. Your spouse must have these documents as well.

1. A valid passport (you do not need to have a passport to apply for immigration, but you must have one when you arrive at a port of entry in Canada).

2. Your national identity card, if applicable.

3. Your birth certificate.

4. Proof of your marital status, such as a marriage certificate, death certificate of spouse, divorce decree, and so on.

5. The birth certificates of all your dependent children whether accompanying you to Canada or not.

6. Proof of all your assets. These might include letters from your banker, bank statements, certificates of deposit, share certificates, title deeds, business ownership papers, and so on.

7. Proof of any assets you might have in Canada.

8. Court documents as applicable. An example of such a document is a court order granting you custody of your children if you are divorced.

9. Adoption documents, if applicable, relating to any adopted children.

10. All your degrees, diplomas, educational certificates, apprenticeship certificates, professional membership certificates or cards, trade qualification documents, and so on. This is for all levels of education, including schools and universities.

11. If you are applying as an Independent Applicant for employment in Canada and have a relative in Canada, documents showing the relationship of your relative to yourself. These might include copies of marriage and birth certificates of yourself and your relative as well as a copy of your relative's Canadian Citizenship card or Record Of Landing.

12. If you are applying in the Entrepreneur, Investor or Self-Employed categories, business registration certificates, income tax returns, etc.

13. Original letters of employment from past employers stating the duration of employment, the dates of employment, the conditions of employment, salaries and fringe benefits paid, and the exact nature of your duties.

14. Original offers of employment in Canada that you might have, which should contain all the information outlined above.

15. Police clearance certificates for yourself, your spouse, and any dependent children accompanying you to Canada who are over 18. Normally, the Immigration authorities will advise you during the processing of your application if such certificates are required. There is no need to submit police certificates with your application, unless requested to do so. However, if you have resided in a foreign country for longer than six (6) months, you will probably have to provide a police clearance certificate from that country.

Filling in the gaps

Some comments should be made about the documents required above. Make every effort to provide all the documents necessary, but do not be alarmed if you cannot obtain all documents, with certain exceptions. An example of an exception is your passport, which you *must* obtain before leaving for Canada.

However, if, for example, you do not have evidence of a degree you obtained twenty years ago, do not despair. First, write to the college or university you attended and ask for a copy of your degree or other verification. If you are not able to obtain it for whatever reason, simply tell the immigration officer you do not have the degree certificate and your efforts to obtain a copy have failed. The officer will normally continue with the processing of your application.

In some countries birth certificates are not obtained by parents and not usually required in one's life. If you do not have a birth certificate, make sure you have a passport or school-leaving certificate, which might be sufficient.

If, however, you or your spouse have a relative in Canada, then you may have to produce your birth certificate and that of your relative in order to prove your relationship to your relative. But often school certificates or other documentation showing your father's or mother's name may be sufficient. If you believe you may have difficulty proving a relationship, an immigration consultant may be able to advise you of the documentation you require, depending on your country of origin.

CONTACTING THE IMMIGRATION OFFICE

Once you have gathered all the above material, you are ready to contact or write to the nearest Canadian Immigration office.

At the end of this chapter you will find a list of toll-free telephone numbers from countries world-wide by which you can contact the Canadian government information service, or if you are on the Internet, visit *www.canada.gc/directories/infor-e.html*, or phone 1-800-O-Canada.

REPLY FROM IMMIGRATION

The reply you receive from Immigration will vary, depending on which office you contact. At the present time, Regional

Processing Centres are being established which will process applications from several different areas or countries. For example, the Canadian Consulate in Buffalo, New York, is now processing all applications from within the United States. The Canadian High Commission in London, England, will be handling all applications from the United Kingdom as well as some countries in the Middle East. So don't be surprised if you are asked to submit your application to a quite unexpected location.

The instructions you receive concerning the submission of your application and the documentation required will also vary from office to office. For example, the Canadian High Commission in Singapore requests virtually no supporting documentation while the Canadian High Commission in Hong Kong insists on receiving every conceivable document along with the application for permanent residence.

You must therefore pay particular attention to the instructions you receive with your application forms and follow those instructions carefully. Not to do so can severely delay the processing of your application. For example, certain offices will return your application and all supporting documentation without considering your application if even one document is missing.

However, whatever office you contact, you will receive the basic Application for Permanent Residence in Canada.

THE APPLICATION FOR PERMANENT RESIDENCE

The **Application for Permanent Residence** is known as form IMM 8. It is four pages long and contains 34 questions. It is a standard application form that is used by all Canadian Immigration offices. A sample is reproduced in Figure 10.

You might receive additional forms that you are required to complete. For example, all applications in Hong Kong must be accompanied by a complete **Family Composition Information** form. If you receive any such forms, you must fill them in and return them with your Application for Permanent Residence.

First, I suggest you read the form carefully to familiarise yourself with the questions. As you can see, the form is not difficult or complicated and asks simple questions.

- **However, your entire future could be altered by the way you fill in this form.**

■◆■ Citizenship and   Citoyenneté et
      Immigration Canada   Immigration Canada

IMMIGRATION
Canada

Table of Contents

Application Kit for Independents

Section One:
General Instructions

This document has been designed for the client's
ease of use. It is not a legal document; for legal
information, please refer to the *Immigration Act*,
1976, and *Regulations*,1978.

Aussi disponible en français

Fig. 10.   Application for Permanent Residence in Canada
(Form IMM 8).

How to Apply to Immigrate to Canada

1 Collect the documents you need to support your application. These are listed in **Section Three/ Appendix C: Checklist**. The **Checklist** will tell you how many copies of the application form the visa office requires. It will also tell you which documents must be originals and which should be photocopies, and whether a certified translation in English or French is required.

2 You, your spouse (if applicable) and each dependent child aged 18 or over (whether accompanying you or not) must complete a separate **Immigrant Application Form (Application for Permanent Residence in Canada)** (IMM 0008), found in **Section Two** (see **Important Words to Know** in the Guide for a definition of "dependent children"). This kit provides only one application form. Before you start to fill it in, ensure you make enough photocopies.

You, your spouse (if applicable) and each dependent child aged 18 or over (whether accompanying you or not) must also complete the **Additional Family Information** form (IMM 5406). It is very important that you list on this form any other children (even if they are already permanent residents of Canada or Canadian **Immigrant Application Form** (IMM 0008). This includes married children and any of your children who have been adopted by others or are in the custody of an ex-spouse.

This kit provides only one form. Before you start to fill it in, ensure you make enough photocopies.

Detailed instructions for completing the forms are provided in the following pages under **How to Complete the Forms**. Do not leave any blanks. Do not forget to sign and date your forms.

3 Use the **Checklist** to verify that you have all of the required documents. It is important to note that the visa office may request additional information at any time during the application process.

4 You, your spouse (if applicable) and each of your dependents, whether they are accompanying you to Canada or not, must undergo a medical examination by a designated physician. Use the instructions in **Section Three/Appendix D: Medical Instructions**.

5 Obtain a police certificate/clearance from every country in which you or your dependents aged 18 years or over have resided for six months or longer since reaching the age of 18. You will find instructions in **Section Three/Appendix E: Obtaining Police Certificates/Clearances**.

6 Use the instructions in **Section Three/Appendix F: Immigration Fee Schedule** to calculate the fees you must send with your application. Do not mail cash.

7 Submit your completed application to the address indicated in the **Checklist**. Print your name and address on the top left-hand side of the envelope.

8 If mailing, ensure that your envelope has sufficient postage. The Post Office will return your application to you if it does not have sufficient postage.

How to Complete the Forms

 Immigrant Application Form (Application for Permanent Residence in Canada) **(IMM 0008)**

There is only one application form in this kit. Before you start to complete it, make a photocopy for each person who needs to submit an individual form. All persons 18 or over (whether accompanying you to Canada or not) must complete an individual application form.

The **Immigrant Application Form** (IMM 0008) is found in **Section Two: The Forms/Appendix A: Immigrant Application Form**. Use these instructions to fill it in. You must answer all questions. If you leave any sections blank, your application will be returned to you for completion and processing will be delayed. If any sections do not apply to you, please answer "NOT APPLICABLE".

> **Use a black pen or typewriter. Print in block letters.**

At the top of the form, please indicate your preferred language for receiving correspondence and for being interviewed.

Also, indicate whether the principal applicant or a dependent aged 18 years or older is completing the form If you are married, either you or your spouse, but not both of you, may be the principal applicant. Once you decide who the principal applicant is, the other spouse and each dependent aged 18 years or older should check the dependent box.

Part A – Personal Details

Part A asks for personal information about you and all of your dependents, whether or not they are immigrating to Canada with you.

1. a) Print your full **family name (surname)** as it appears on your passport or on the official documents that will be used for obtaining your passport.

    b) Print all of your **given name(s)** (first, second or more). Do not use initials. Again, print it as it appears on your passport or on the official documents that will be used for obtaining your passport.

    c) Write your **full name in your own native language script**. Include your family name and all given names.

2. Print any **other names** you have used, such as your name before marriage, your name during a previous marriage, a nickname or an alias. Include pet or familiar names.

3. Check the appropriate box to indicate **male** or **female**.

4. Print your **height** either in centimeters or in feet and inches.

5. Check the appropriate box to indicate the **colour of your eyes.**

6. a) Print your **date of birth** by day/month/year.

    b) Print your **place of birth** giving the city, town or village (or nearest community) in which you were born.

    c) Print your **country of birth**. This is the name of the country in which you were born.

7. Print your **country of citizenship**. If you have more than one country of citizenship, give details on a separate page.

8. a) Print your **mailing address**. This is the address we will use to mail correspondence regarding your application. As well, please write your mailing address in your own native language script. If you need more room, use a separate page.

   b) Print your complete **telephone number**, including country and area codes.

   c) If you have access to a **facsimile** machine, print the fax number including country and area codes.

   d) Print your current **residential address.** Please write this address in your native language script. If you need more room, use a separate page.

9. a) Check only one box to indicate your **present marital status.** You must provide proof of your marital status. If you are divorced, or if your previous spouse died, and you are now remarried, check the "married" box and attach an explanatory note.

   b) If you have been married more than once, check "yes" and indicate in the space provided the number of times that you have been married. If you have never been married or married only once, check "no". You must provide your current marriage certificate, and divorce or death certificate(s) for all previous spouses.

10. a) Print your **passport number**.

    b) Print the name of the **country which issued your passport**.

    c) Print **the date your passport expires** by day/month/year.

    d) Print your **identity card number**, if applicable.

11. a) Print the title of your **current occupation**.

    b) Print the title of the **occupation in which you intend to work in Canada**.

12. **Formal education**. Indicate the total number of years that you have attended and successfully completed.

13. Check the box that indicates the highest **level of education** you have successfully completed:

    - **Secondary** education is the level of schooling after elementary and before college, university, or other formal training.

    - **Formal trade certificate/apprenticeship** refers to completed training in an occupation such as "auto mechanic".

    - **Non-university certificate or diploma** refers to training in a profession that requires formal education but not at the university level (for example, dental technicians or engineering technicians).

    - **Some university, but no degree**, refers to completion of some university courses but not enough to obtain a degree.

    - **Bachelor's degree** refers to your first university degree, such as a Bachelor of Arts, Education, Engineering or other professional field.

    - **Some post-graduate studies, but no degree**, means you have obtained a Bachelor's degree and completed some studies at the post-graduate level.

    - **Master's degree** is your first post-graduate degree.

    - **Ph.D.** is the highest university degree.

14. Print your **native language** (the first language you spoke).

15. Read each of the statements (A to H) in this question carefully. Answer "yes" or "no" on behalf of yourself and your dependents. If you answer "yes" to any question, provide full details in the space provided. Use a separate page if necessary.

16. This question asks for personal details about your **dependents**, whether they are accompanying you to Canada or not. The first column is for the details about your spouse. If you have never been or are not currently married, print "NOT APPLICABLE" in the first box. The remaining columns are for details about your dependent children – your son(s) and daughter(s) – starting with the oldest. You must include all of your dependents (who are not already permanent residents of Canada or Canadian citizens), whether they intend to immigrate with you or not. If you have more than three dependents, attach a separate page with the same information provided in the same order.

    - Print your dependent's family name (surname).
    - Print your dependent's given names. Include all given names. Do not use initials.
    - Print your dependent's date of birth by day/month/year.
    - Check the appropriate box to indicate if your dependent is male or female.
    - Print the place of birth giving the city, town or village (or nearest community) in which your dependent was born.
    - Print the country of birth. This is the name of the country in which your dependent was born.
    - Print the country where your dependents have resident status.
    - Print the country of citizenship of your dependent. If he/she has more than one country of citizenship, give details on a separate page.
    - Check the appropriate box to indicate your dependent's current marital status. Use the same categories listed in Question 9a). You must provide proof of his/her marital status. If any of your dependents are divorced, or if their previous spouse died, and they are now remarried, check the "married" box. You must provide the marriage and divorce certificates, or death certificate(s) for all of your dependents' previous spouses.
    - Relationship. The first column is "spouse"; the others will read "son" or "daughter".
    - Check the appropriate box to indicate whether or not your spouse and/or dependent(s) will accompany you to Canada. "Accompany" means the person will immigrate to Canada within the validity of the visa but may arrive in Canada after you.
    - Print the passport number for each dependent.
    - Print the name of the country that issued the passport.
    - Indicate the date on which the passport is due to expire, by day/month/year.
    - Print your dependent's identity card number, if applicable.
    - Print the title of your dependent's current occupation. This may include "homemaker", "student" or "dependent child", as applicable.
    - Indicate the total number of years of formal education for each dependent.
    - Indicate the level of education successfully completed for each dependent. Use the categories listed in Question 13.
    - If your dependent is fluent in English, check the appropriate box. If not, check "no".
    - If your dependent is fluent in French, check the appropriate box. If not, check "no".
    - Print your dependent's native language (the first language he/she spoke).

17. Use the instructions in **Section Three/Appendix C: Checklist** and enclose in an envelope the required number of photographs of yourself, your spouse (if applicable), and each person listed in item 16, whether they are accompanying you to Canada or not. All photographs must have been taken within the past six months and must be identified by printing the person's name on the back of the photograph. Attach the envelope to the form in a way that allows it to be removed (for example, a staple rather than glue).

Part B – Skills and Qualifications

At the top of the page, in the box indicating "Name of applicant/dependent completing form", print the name of the person to whom the following information applies:

1. **Language:** This question asks about your ability to speak, read, and write Canada's official languages. Check the box that best describes your ability to speak English and French. Use the following definitions:

   Fluently: Speak, read and write with ease in a range of social and work situations, and no difficulty communicating in a professional capacity.

   Well: Speak, read and write well in a range of social and work situations.

   With difficulty: Speak, read and write in a very limited way.

   Not at all: No ability to communicate in this language at any level.

2. **Education:** Print the number of years of formal schooling successfully completed in each of the categories indicated.

3. **Post-secondary education:** Print the details of university, college, and/or apprenticeship training. Begin with the most recent program completed. Use an additional page if necessary.

4. **Work history:** Print the details of your work history since your 18th birthday. Begin with your most recent job. Include work you have done in other countries. You must account for every month since your 18th birthday. If you did not work for any period during that time, enter what you were doing (for example, unemployed, studying or travelling). Use an additional page if necessary. Start with the date you began the job by month/year and the date it ended by month/year. In the next column, print the full name of your employer (do not use abbreviations). In the next column, print the city and country in which you worked at that job. Then, print your occupation with the employer (be specific: for example, rather than "public servant" print "financial clerk"). If the job was part time, put a check mark in this column. In the last column print how much you earned per month.

5. **Contact address:** Print the name and address of any close relative (see **Important Words to Know in the Guide**), employer, or organization willing to assist you in Canada. If more than one relative is a permanent resident of Canada or Canadian citizen living in Canada, print the name, address, and relationship of the relative most ready to assist you. If none, print "NOT APPLICABLE".

6. Print the **relationship** of any person that you name in box 5.

7. **Destination in Canada:**

   a) Print the name of the **city** or **town** in which you intend to live in Canada.

   b) Print the name of the **province** in which you intend to live in Canada.

8. **Funds:** Indicate how much money (in Canadian dollars) you will be bringing with you to Canada and the value of any property you own. Do not list jewellery, cars and other personal assets. You must provide proof that you have enough money to maintain yourself and your dependents until you become self-supporting in Canada.

9. **Debts and Obligations:** List the amount of all loans, debts, and financial obligations, including fees owing to lawyers and consultants and alimony and child-support payments, in Canadian dollars. Use an extra page if necessary.

10. **Addresses:** Print all of your addresses since your 18th birthday. Do not use post office (P.O.) box addresses. Give a complete address including the street, town or city, province or region, and country. If there was no street or street number, explain exactly the location of the house or building. You must account for every month. Use an additional page if necessary.

Part C

1. Print details of any **organizations or associations** of which you have been a member since your 18th birthday. Include the full name of any political, social, youth, student or vocational organizations and any trade unions or professional associations. List any voluntary or compulsory military service, including rank, unit and location of service. If you did not belong to any organizations or perform military service, print "NOT APPLICABLE" in the space provided.

2. For each of your **parents**, starting with your father, print their full names (including surname and given names), their dates of birth, and the city or town and the country in which they were born. If either of your parents is deceased, indicate the date of death by day/month/year.

3. **Authority to disclose personal information.** Complete this section only if you want us to release the information on your application to someone other than yourself. Privacy laws prevent Citizenship and Immigration Canada from discussing your application with anyone else unless you give us permission to do so. If you have a representative (for example, a relative, friend, lawyer or consultant) helping you to complete the application process, and you authorize us to discuss your case with him or her, print the representative's name and address in this section and sign on the line provided.

4. **Declaration of Applicant.** Read the statements carefully. Sign and date on the lines provided. By signing, you certify that you fully understand the questions asked and that the information you have provided is complete, truthful, and correct. If you do not sign, the application will be returned to you.

5. **Solemn Declaration.** Do not complete this section unless you are asked to do so by a visa officer at an interview.

> It is an offence under the *Immigration Act* knowingly to make a false or misleading statement in connection with an application for permanent residence in Canada.

IMMIGRANT APPLICATION FORM - *INDEPENDENT*
(APPLICATION FOR PERMANENT RESIDENCE IN CANADA)

Date of receipt stamp at post

Indicate your choice of language:

For correspondence	For interview
English French	English French

FOR OFFICE USE ONLY
Office file number (or IMM 1343 Case Label)

I AM ▶ The principal applicant **OR** A dependant aged 18 years or older

NOTE: ALL PERSONS AGE 18 YEARS OR OLDER MUST COMPLETE THIS FORM.

PART A   PERSONAL DETAILS

1 a) My family name (surname) is: b) Given name(s):

c) My full name written in my native language or script (for example, Arabic, Cyrillic, Chinese, Korean, Japanese characters or Chinese commercial/telegraphic code) is:

2 All other names I have used including name(s) before marriage (if applicable):

3 Sex   Male   Female

4 Height   CM or   Feet   Inches

5 Eye colour   Blue   Green   Grey   Black   Brown   Hazel (yellowish brown)   Other _____

6 a) My date of birth is: Day Month Year   b) Place of birth (city or town)   c) Country of birth   **7** I am a citizen of:

8 a) My mailing address is: b) Telephone number   d) My current residential address is:

c) Facsimile number

9 a) My present marital status is: Never married   Engaged   Married   Widowed   Separated   Divorced   Annulled marriage

b) I have been married more than once: Yes   No   If "Yes", state number of times ▶ _____

10 a) My passport number is   b) Country of issue   c) Date of expiry Day Month Year   d) Identity card number

11 a) Current occupation   b) My intended occupation in Canada is:

12 Total years of formal education   **13** Indicate your level of education   Secondary or less   Formal trade certificate/apprenticeship   Non-university certificate, or diploma   Some university, but no degree   Bachelor's degree   Some post-graduate studies, but no degree   Master's degree   Ph. D.   **14** My native language is:

15 Have you or has any one of the persons in question (16) PART A ever: (Check "Yes" or "No")

A. Been convicted of or currently charged with a crime or offence in any country?   Yes   No

B. Previously sought refugee status in Canada or applied for an immigrant or visitor visa?   Yes   No

C. Been refused refugee status in, or an immigrant or visitor visa to, Canada or any other country, or have been refused a CSQ to Quebec?   Yes   No

D. Been refused admission to, or ordered to leave, Canada or any other country?   Yes   No

E. Whether in peace or war, have you ever been involved in the deportation of civilians or in the commission of a war crime or crime against humanity, such as: willful killing, torture, attacks upon, enslavement, starvation or other inhumane acts against civilians or prisoners of war?   Yes   No

F. Used, planned or advocated or been associated with a group that used, uses or advocated the use of armed struggle or violence to reach political, religious or social objectives?   Yes   No

G. Been detained or incarcerated?   Yes   No

H. Had any serious disease or physical or mental disorder?   Yes   No

If the answer to any of the above is "Yes", provide details here:

PERSONAL DETAILS OF ALL MY DEPENDENTS WHETHER ACCOMPANYING ME OR NOT (If you require additional space, attach separate sheet.)

16	Spouse	Dependant 1	Dependant 2	Dependant 3
Family name				
Given name(s)				
Date of birth	Day Month Year	Day Month Year	Day Month Year	Day Month Year
Sex	☐ Male ☐ Female	☐ Male ☐ Female	☐ Male ☐ Female	☐ Male ☐ Female
Place of birth (city or town)				
Country of birth				
Country of residence				
Country of citizenship				
Marital status (Use one of the categories listed in 9a)	Married	Never married	Never married	Never married
Relationship to me	**SPOUSE**			
Will accompany me to Canada	☐ Yes ☐ No	☐ Yes ☐ No	☐ Yes ☐ No	☐ Yes ☐ No
Passport number ▶				
Country of issue ▶				
Date of expiry ▶	Day Month Year	Day Month Year	Day Month Year	Day Month Year
Identity card number				
Current occupation				
Years of formal education				
Level of education attained (Use categories in 13)	Secondary or less	Secondary or less	Secondary or less	Secondary or less
Fluent in English	☐ Yes ☐ No	☐ Yes ☐ No	☐ Yes ☐ No	☐ Yes ☐ No
Fluent in French	☐ Yes ☐ No	☐ Yes ☐ No	☐ Yes ☐ No	☐ Yes ☐ No
Native language				

17 **PRINCIPAL APPLICANT:** Attach an envelope containing photographs of yourself and each person listed in Item 16, as requested in Appendix C of the kit.

ALL PHOTOGRAPHS MUST HAVE BEEN TAKEN WITHIN THE PAST 6 MONTHS AND MUST BE IDENTIFIED BY WRITING THE PERSON'S NAME AND DATE OF BIRTH ON THE BACK OF THE PHOTOGRAPH.

FOR OFFICIAL USE ONLY

Name of applicant/dependent completing form

PART B — SKILLS AND QUALIFICATIONS

1 | LANGUAGE

ABILITY IN ENGLISH:				ABILITY IN FRENCH:			
SPEAK ☐ Fluently	☐ Well	☐ With difficulty	☐ Not at all	**SPEAK** ☐ Fluently	☐ Well	☐ With difficulty	☐ Not at all
READ ☐ Fluently	☐ Well	☐ With difficulty	☐ Not at all	**READ** ☐ Fluently	☐ Well	☐ With difficulty	☐ Not at all
WRITE ☐ Fluently	☐ Well	☐ With difficulty	☐ Not at all	**WRITE** ☐ Fluently	☐ Well	☐ With difficulty	☐ Not at all

2 | EDUCATION

My education (indicate number of years of school successfully completed):

Years of elementary/ primary school	Years of secondary/ high school	Years of university/ college	Years of formal apprenticeship/training

3 | DETAILS OF MY POST SECONDARY EDUCATION (including university, college and apprenticeship training)

Dates From M Y	To M Y	Name of institution	City and country	Type of certificate or diploma issued

4 | MY WORK HISTORY *SINCE MY 18th BIRTHDAY* (Continue on a separate page if necessary)

Dates From M Y	To M Y	Name of employer (Write name in full; do not use abbreviations)	City and country	My occupation	Part time (✓)	Gross monthly salary
					☐	
					☐	
					☐	
					☐	

5 | The following person, employer or organization in Canada has offered to assist me after arrival (Name and address and copy of job offer, if you have one)

6 Relationship to me of person named in 5	**7** Destination in Canada		**8** How much money will you bring with you?
	a) City or town	b) Province	$

9 | I have the following debts or legal obligations (for example, child support payments) owing to: (Give name of person(s) or organization)   Total debts (Amount)

10 | *SINCE MY 18th BIRTHDAY* I HAVE LIVED AT THE FOLLOWING ADDRESSES

Dates From M Y	To M Y	Street and number	City or town	Country

PART C

1 Since my 18th birthday, I have been (or still am) a member of, or associated with, the following political, social, youth, student or vocational organizations, trade unions or professional associations. Include military service (show rank, unit and location of service in last column)

Dates				Name and address of organization	Type of organization	Position held (if any)
From		To				
M	Y	M	Y			

2 MY PARENTS

Father's full name

Date of birth			City or town of birth:	Country of birth:	If deceased, give date:		
Day	Month	Year			Day	Month	Year

Mother's full name before marriage:

Date of birth			City or town of birth:	Country of birth:	If deceased, give date:		
Day	Month	Year			Day	Month	Year

3 AUTHORITY TO DISCLOSE PERSONAL INFORMATION

A. I understand that the Canadian Government will contact any government authority, including police, judicial and state authorities in all countries in which I have resided, to seek the release to the Canadian Government authorities of all records and information that they may possess on my behalf concerning any investigations, arrests, charges, trials, convictions and sentences. I understand that this information will be used to assist in evaluating my suitability for admission to Canada or remaining in Canada, pursuant to Canadian immigration legislation.

B. I also authorize the release of information from my Immigration records to: (check one or more)

☐ The individual named hereinafter: _____

(Name of individual)

☐ My sponsor

☐ My representative in Canada (if any)

_____   _____
Name of individual   Name of firm

Day	Month	Year

_____
Signature of applicant   Date

4 DECLARATION OF APPLICANT

• I declare that the information I have given in this application is truthful, complete and correct.

• I understand that any false statements or concealment of a material fact may result in my exclusion from Canada and may be grounds for my prosecution or removal.

• I understand all the foregoing statements, having asked for and obtained an explanation on every point which was not clear to me.

Day	Month	Year

_____
Signature of applicant   Date

DO NOT COMPLETE THE FOLLOWING SECTION NOW. YOU MAY BE ASKED TO SIGN IN THE PRESENCE OF A REPRESENTATIVE OF THE CANADIAN GOVERNMENT OR AN OFFICIAL APPOINTED BY THE CANADIAN GOVERNMENT.

5 SOLEMN DECLARATION

I, _____ , solemnly declare that the information I have given in the foregoing application is truthful, complete and correct, and I make this solemn declaration conscientiously believing it to be true and knowing that it is of the same force and effect as if made under oath.

_____
Signature of applicant

Declared before me at _____ this ____ day of _____ of the year

INTERPRETER DECLARATION

I, _____ , do solemnly declare that I have faithfully and accurately interpreted in the _____ language the content of this application and any related forms to the person concerned.

I have been informed by the person concerned, and I do verily believe, that he/she completely understands the nature and effect of these forms, and I make this solemn declaration conscientiously believing it to be true and knowing that it is of the same force and effect as is made under oath.

_____
Signature of interpreter

_____
Signature of the official of Government of Canada

The information you provide on this form is collected under the authority of the *Immigration Act* and will be used for the purpose of assessing your application for permanent residence in Canada. This information will be retained in the Personal Information Bank EIC PPU 015 entitled Immigrant Case File. Under the provisions of the *Privacy Act* and the *Access to Information Act* individuals have the right to protection of and access to their personal information. Instructions for obtaining information are provided in InfoSource, a copy of which is located in all Citizenship and Immigration Offices.

ADDITIONAL FAMILY INFORMATION

Complete **ALL** names in English and in your native language (for example, Arabic, Cyrillic, Chinese, Chinese commercial/telegraphic code, Korean, or Japanese characters). If additional space is required attach a separate sheet.

SECTION A

Name	Relationship	Date of birth Day Month Year	Place of birth	Marital status	Present address
	Applicant				
	Spouse SEE NOTE 1				
	Mother				
	Father				

NOTE 1: If no spouse is listed in Section A, read and sign below.

I certify that I do not have a spouse, former spouse or ex-spouse.

Signature | Day Month Year | Date

SECTION B   CHILDREN (Include ALL sons and daughters, including ALL adopted and step-children, regardless of age or place of residence)

Name	Relationship SEE NOTE 2	Date of birth Day Month Year	Place of birth	Marital status	Present address

NOTE 2: If no children are listed in Section B, read and sign below.

I certify that I do not have any children, either natural or adopted.

Signature | Day Month Year | Date

SECTION C   BROTHERS AND SISTERS (Including half - and step-brothers and sisters)

Name	Relationship	Date of birth Day Month Year	Place of birth	Marital status	Present address

SECTION D   CERTIFICATION

I certify that the information contained on this document is complete, accurate and factual. I also realize that once this document has been completed and signed that it will form part of my Immigration Record and will be used to verify my family details on future applications.

Signature | Day Month Year | Date

Additional Family Information (IMM 5406)

This form is intended to gather additional information about your family and is found in **Section Two/ Appendix B**. There is only one form in this kit. Before you start to complete it, make a photocopy for each person who needs to submit an individual form. You must answer all questions. If any sections do not apply to you, please answer "NOT APPLICABLE".

You, your spouse (if applicable), and each dependent child aged 18 or over (whether accompanying you or not) must complete this form. It is very important that you list on this form any other children (even if they are already permanent residents of Canada or Canadian citizens) that you, your spouse or your dependent children might have who are not included in your **Immigrant Application Form** (IMM 0008). This includes married children and any of your children who have been adopted by others, or are in the custody of an ex-spouse.

The information you provide is collected under the authority of the *Immigration Act* to determine if you may be admitted to Canada as an immigrant. It will be stored in Personal Information Bank number EIC PPU 015. It is protected and accessible under the provisions of the *Privacy Act* and the *Access to Information Act.*

Completing the Application for Permanent Residence

The information you provide on the Application for Permanent Residence form will be the main determining factor in the approval or rejection of your application for immigration. Fill it out using the utmost care, providing as much detail as possible and, as always, being absolutely truthful.

I advise you to photocopy the application form when you receive it and use the copy to practise on before finalising the actual application. Generally, there is not a great deal of difference between the application forms provided by different offices.

The instructions in the Application Kit are pretty clear, but I would offer you the following advice concerning the completion of your application.

Firstly, you should complete all questions. If any question is not applicable to you, simply insert 'Not Applicable' or 'N/A' in the space provided, but be sure to answer every question.

Please note as well that you must indicate your language preference (English or French) for correspondence and interview in the appropriate box at the top of the form, and indicate if you are the **Principal Applicant** (the person whose qualifications are to be assessed) or if you are a **Dependant** of the Principal Applicant. As noted above, the **application varies slightly from office to office**, but here are my comments on the basic questions.

Name
State your surname (family name), first name, and middle name, in that order. You need also to provide your name in your native script if applicable.

Other names
In this space you should write any other names under which you have been known. If you are a married woman, your maiden name should be included. If you are divorced or have been married more than once, your previous married name(s) should be included. You need not include nicknames, unless people know you only by your nickname and not your real name, or if your nickname is included in any job references.

Sex, height and eye colour
These questions are self-explanatory.

Date of birth
Insert your date of birth. Note that in some countries, for example the United States, dates are written differently with the month first, followed by the day and year. You should follow the exact format given in the form, that is, day, month and year. If you do not know your exact date of birth and have no way to find out, insert the word 'about' before the birth date.

Place of birth and country of birth
Insert the name of the city/town and country where you were born.

Citizenship
Insert the name of the country of which you are a citizen. If you are not the citizen of any country, you should insert 'State-less'.

Some applicants are dual citizens due to naturalisation or birth. You may pick one country, usually the country on whose passport you travel, or declare both countries.

Present mailing address
You should give your complete permanent mailing address, including, your apartment or house number, apartment or house name, street name, city, state or province, country and postal code. This is the address at which you are presently receiving mail.

Alongside that you need to provide your telephone number (and fax number if you have one) including the area code.

If your current residential address is different from your mailing address, you need to provide the address at which you are actually living.

If you engage a consultant in Canada to handle your application, he or she will receive all correspondence from Immigration, including your visas when issued.

Marital status
You should tick the appropriate box for your marital status. Note that 'unmarried (never married)' means that you have not gone through any form of marriage in any country at any time in your life. You must also indicate if you have been previously married and how often.

Date of marriage
You should state the date and the place you were married, if applicable. You need mention only the city/town and country, not the name of the church in which you were married.

Number of marriages
If you have been married more than once, indicate the number of times. Remember, if you have been married more than once, you should attach copies of your divorce papers or spouse's death certificate to your application.

Dependants
Include the names, relationships, dates of birth, places of birth and citizenship of all your children and your spouse's children whether married or single, in descending order of birth, and indicate if they intend to accompany you to Canada. You must include the names of all your unmarried children whether or not they intend to accompany or follow you to Canada.

Passport particulars
Enter the number of your passport or travel document, the date it was issued, the expiration date, and the country it was issued by. Note that this applies not only to you but also to all your unmarried children, whether or not they will accompany you to Canada. The country of issue is the name of the country on whose passport you travel, and not the place where you obtained that passport. You do not have to have a passport when applying for immigration to Canada, and your visa can be issued before you have a passport, but you must have a passport when you arrive at a port of entry to Canada along with your visa.

Many countries do not issue identity cards, but some do. If you have one, insert the number of your card.

Current and intended occupation
Keep in mind that your intended occupation has to appear on the General List of Occupations to be approved, unless you are applying within the business categories.

Usually, your present and intended occupation will be the same. However, if you were qualified and employed some years ago in an occupation in demand, while current occupation is not presently in demand, you should of course apply in your former occupation.

It is very important that you pick you job occupation as carefully as possible. Go through the list carefully, checking to see in which occupations you are qualified. Go back to the various lists of occupations. **Choose that occupation you are qualified for and might work in when you are in Canada**. You do not have to put down only one occupation. If you are qualified in more than one occupation, such as Accountant or Budget Accountant or Bank Branch Accountant, then put them all down. You should receive consideration for the occupation with the highest Occupational Demand points.

Be as specific as possible. For example, if you are an Electrical Engineer, do not put down simply 'engineer', as there are chemical, civil, structural, design, electronic, industrial, mechanical, tool, metallurgical, mining, aerospace and other engineers as well. Each of them could have different Occupational Demand points.

Language ability
You should indicate your ability to speak, read and write Canada's two official languages, English and French. You may estimate your language skills yourself, and you do not normally have to document your ability. However, if you do have certificates indicating your proficiency in English or French, attach them to the application.

You may be tested in your language abilities, unless you are obviously fluent in either language. You do not have to have any proficiency in either of Canada's official languages in order to have your application approved. Obviously, however, it helps your case if you are fluent in either language, as you will normally need one or the other, or both, to live and work in Canada.

If you speak neither English nor French, indicate the language you normally speak. This would normally be your native language. 'Native language' is hard to define, but normally it would mean the language you speak at home or are most proficient in.

Education
You should fill in the boxes according to the number of years you successfully completed in elementary and secondary school, college and formal training.

It is often difficult to distinguish between secondary schooling and primary schooling. In certain countries primary or elementary schooling is only five years, while in others it might be eight. Similarly, in certain countries secondary or high school is only three years; in others it might be seven.

The breakdown is not important. What is important is that you designate the total number of years you went to school. For example, if you went to school for twelve years, you may break it down into seven years of primary school and five years of high school or six years of primary school and six years of high school, according to the system used in the country of your schooling. However, both must add up to twelve to indicate to the immigration officer you went to school for twelve years.

Similarly, put the total number of years you attended college or university in the appropriate box. You need not break this total down by degrees or levels of college or university.

You should also indicate the number of years you completed in formal training. This does not include training you might have had informally from a friend or taught yourself. Usually, training applies only to occupations in trades, such as mechanics and carpenters. Formal Apprenticeship Training refers to a formal programme of instruction which would usually involve both practical and theoretical instruction and the issuance of a certificate or diploma.

You should remember two points when filling out the section on education. First, you must enter only those years you passed. Failed years of education should not be included, as they are not accepted for the allocation of points.

Second, you will have to prove details of your education, through such documents as copies of your diplomas, degrees and certificates. You should put down only those years you actually attended a school, college, university or training programme. If you attended an institution as a part-time student, you may include it on the form, but should indicate it was for part-time studies only.

Fill in the rest of the question with the months and years you started and finished your post-secondary education at each school, college, university or training programme you attended. The name and location of each school, college, university or training programme, the type of educational institution it was, and the name and date of any degree, diploma or certificate issued must be included.

In the section on the type of institution, you need not be too specific. If, for example, you attended a four-year institution granting a bachelor's degree in liberal arts, you need only put the word 'college' or 'university' in response to this question. If you took a formal training course at a factory or manufacturing plant, or had other on-the-job training, you may put down 'apprenticeship' as the type of institution.

Similarly, you need not be too specific in the type and date of certificate or degree or diploma you received. If, for example, you hold a Doctor of Philosophy in English Literature, you need only put the letters 'Ph.D.' in this section.

Work history
List the dates in months and years, the name and address of the employer, your occupation, and your gross monthly earnings for all your jobs over at least the past ten years. You need not limit yourself to only the past ten years, if you have previous relevant experience. In fact, it is recommended that you list your entire work history.

Specify your occupation carefully, as your past experience should be as closely related to your intended occupation in Canada as possible. It is advisable to refer to the Occupational Demand chart for descriptive names of your previous occupations. You should not put your formal title, such as 'Vice President for Asia, including South East Asia', if that is your title, but rather the descriptive title, 'Manager: Sales'.

Your gross monthly earnings should be stated in your local currency. For the most part, Canadian immigration officers are aware of the significance of the salaries paid in local currencies.

Employer or relatives in Canada
List anyone in Canada who is willing and able to help you get settled in Canada. This person may be either a relative or a friend, or, if you already have arranged employment, your prospective employer. If you are a Sponsored Dependant, list the relative in Canada who is helping you immigrate by sponsoring your application. But only list relatives closer than a cousin who are citizens of Canada or permanent residents.

Relationship
You should list the relationship to you of the person named in the previous question, such as brother, friend, prospective employer, etc. If the person is an aunt, uncle, nephew or niece, state clearly the relationship, for example, 'aunt – my father's sister'.

Destination
Fill in the city and province in Canada to which you wish to go. If you have not decided on a city, write the name of the province where you intend to reside.

Assets
I believe it is best to state your assets in terms of Canadian dollars when completing this question.

Indicate in Canadian dollars the approximate value of your home and any other real estate you may own and show any pension you may receive that can be transferred to Canada. In addition, indicate the value of any other valuables you own, such as stocks, bonds, gold, jewellery, antiques, etc. and provide the details.

Debts and obligations
You are required to provide the details of your debts and legal obligations such as child support payments, etc., if any.

Residence background
You should state all the places you have lived during the past ten years, including dates in months and years, and complete addresses. This is for security checks. Start with your oldest address and work down to your present address. Include your actual residence address, and not mailing addresses such as post office boxes.

Clubs/membership
List all the political, social, student and other groups or organisations you have belonged to since your eighteenth birthday.

Parents' particulars
You should fill in your father's and mother's *full* names, date of birth, places of birth, and present addresses, as applicable.

Often, prospective immigrants do not have this information. If that is the case, and the information is not available, insert the word 'Unknown' to any question to which you do not know or have the answer, or indicate approximate dates of birth, e.g. 'About 1934'.

You should make every possible effort to obtain this information before filling out this question. If your relative is deceased, write 'Deceased', and give the date on which he or she died, writing the day, month and year in that order, and the city and country where the death occurred.

Background
You must answer each question by printing either Yes or No. Again, you are reminded to be entirely truthful in your answers. **Please note that these questions apply to your spouse and any dependants accompanying you to Canada**. In addition, you are required to provide details for any question you answer Yes.

Health questions
If you answer 'yes' to this question, it does not mean your application will be refused. Only Canadian immigration doctors can decide which physical or mental disorders and communicable and chronic diseases are grounds for refusal of an application.

Convictions
If you have been convicted of any crime or offence, you may be refused admission into Canada, and your application may be rejected. There are clearly defined legal rules to judge if a person is inadmissible because of convictions.

First, if you have been convicted of very minor offences, such as parking and speeding offences, you need not tick the 'yes' box.

Second, if you have been convicted of a serious offence, you must tick the 'yes' box and provide details.

If you have a conviction, you may still be allowed to immigrate to Canada under a waiver given by the Minister of Immigration. Generally, these are given only after over five years have passed since you finished your sentence, and are able to demonstrate rehabilitation.

If you have been convicted of offences more serious than driving tickets, we suggest you contact a competent Canadian immigration consultant to advise you before applying.

Previous applications
If you previously submitted an application for permanent residence or an application for a visitor's visa, you should indicate 'yes', and indicate below where and when you applied, and the outcome.

If you have submitted a formal application previously and been refused, you must answer 'yes'. Immigration will probably have a record of your previous application and you might be refused, not because of your previous refusal, but because you have been untruthful on your present application.

Don't worry unduly about previous refusals. Certainly a previous refusal does not help your case, but it does not mean your current application will be refused. You may have applied earlier under an entirely different set of regulations, or at a time when you were less qualified.

Refused a visa or admission to Canada or ordered to leave Canada or any other country
A 'yes' answer does not mean your application will be refused. If you have been ordered to leave or you have been deported from any country, or if you have been refused a visa to enter any country, you are advised to contact a Canadian immigration consultant before submitting a new application.

War crimes
This question is self-explanatory.

Photographs
If you are the principal applicant, include three (3) photographs of yourself and, if applicable, of your dependent children under the age of 18 in this space.

If you are the spouse or a dependent child of the applicant over the age of 18, simply include three photographs of yourself only.

Put the photos in a small envelope and staple the envelope to the application, after writing the names and the birth dates on the back of each photo.

Please note carefully that Immigration photographs are not the same as passport photographs. They must meet specific requirements. You should advice your photographer that the photograph must:

- show a full front view of the person's head and shoulders showing full face centred in the middle of the photograph.

- have a plain white background

- be identical (black and white or colour) produced from the same untouched negative, or exposed simultaneously by a split-image or multi-lens camera

- be produced on single weight matte paper.

The photographs must measure:

* between 25mm and 35mm 1″ and $1^3/8$″) from chin to crown
* have a 35mm x 45mm ($1^3/8$″ x $1^3/4$″) finished size.

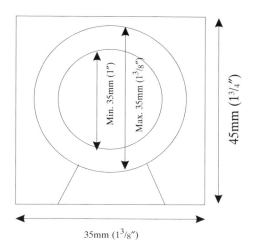

35mm ($1^3/8$″)

Authority to disclose personal information
Read this section carefully. If you want information to be released to your representative or to your relative in Canada, you would tick the first box and indicate the person's name.

Similarly, if you are applying as a Sponsored Dependant of a relative in Canada, you would probably want to tick the second box as well.

If you are represented by an immigration consultant or lawyer, you would normally want to tick the third box and indicate the name of the representative and the name of the firm.

In any event, don't forget to sign and date this section.

Declaration
Read this Declaration and Warning very carefully, keeping in mind that all information provided on the application must be complete and factual.

In addition, should your marital status change, your number of dependants change or any of your answers change at any time prior to immigrating to Canada, you must report any such changes to Immigration and perhaps delay your departure. Once again, don't forget to sign and date this section.

Solemn declaration and interpreter declaration
Do **not** complete these questions. This will be done by the Immigration officer at the time of your interview, if necessary.

SUBMITTING YOUR COMPLETED APPLICATION

Remember, either you or your spouse can apply for permanent residence. Refer back to Chapter 3. Did you decide to have your spouse apply instead of you? If so, then your spouse should fill in the principal Application for Permanent Residence.

Second, do not hesitate to attach additional sheets if necessary. You should put your name on each additional sheet, and indicate the question to which you are referring. Remember to securely fasten the sheets to the form.

Third, I suggest you use a typewriter or computer. The appearance of the application form is important, as you will want to make a favourable first impression on the officer, and it is your form that he or she will first see.

Fourth, your spouse and unmarried children over 19 years of age must complete separate application forms. If you do not have forms for them, write to the Canadian Embassy, High Commission or Consulate that sent you the Application for Permanent Residence and request additional copies. Or, simply make a good photocopy of your application before completion. This does not mean that your spouse and unmarried children are not being dealt with under your application. However, security checks are conducted on your spouse and your children over 19 accompanying you to Canada.

Documenting the application

You should also include certain attachments, *even if these have not been specifically requested.* Do not send originals of any documents especially important ones such as your passport and birth certificates. But do attach copies of your degrees, diplomas and educational certificates, letters from past employers, and any offer of employment in Canada.

- *Most important!* Be certain to attach a separate sheet of paper providing a complete description of your occupational duties over the years. You are advised to attach a similar job description for your spouse. These job descriptions are essential! Immigration officers have to be satisfied that you are (or your spouse is) qualified in an intended occupation. They do this by considering your practical experience in relation to thousands of detailed job descriptions. It is impossible to reproduce these thousands of job descriptions in this book, but to give you an idea of the detail contained in these job descriptions, the NOC (National Occupational Classification) job descriptions of a few occuptions are included. These descriptions should provide you with an idea of the detail you need to go into in preparing the job description for your particular occupation.

When you are satisfied that the application is properly completed and documented, mail or take it back to the Canadian High Commission, Embassy or Consulate you received it from.

CAUTIONS

1. I will deal with the subject of payment of fees to third parties in Chapter 10. You might want to refer to that chapter before completing the application form. Professional advice and a professionally completed application can go a long way in assisting the favourable outcome of your application and often make the difference between acceptance and refusal.

2. You should take no irreversible steps, such as giving up your employment or disposing of your properties, until you have been issued with the **Immigrant Visa and Record of Landing.**

3. I would remind you again to inform the Canadian High Commission, Embassy or Consulate you are applying to if any of the following occur to you before you leave for Canada, but after you have submitted the application form:

   - You become engaged, married, widowed, separated or divorced.

   - You or your spouse gives birth to a child.

- Any of your answers change from 'no' to 'yes', such as if you are convicted of a serious offence.

Failure to inform the Canadian immigration office dealing with your case could have very serious consequences in the future. For example, if you get married after receiving your Canadian Immigration Visa and Record of Landing and enter Canada without informing immigration officials of your change in marital status, you could be deported from Canada. Deportation would not occur for getting married, but rather for not informing Immigration of the fact.

Once you have mailed in your application, you will have to wait. It will be dealt with according to the established priority system.

CANADIAN GOVERNMENT INFORMATION

When you need information on the government of Canada, call toll-free or visit the website *www.canada.gc.ca*

The following is a list of toll-free numbers for accessing 1 800 O-Canada outside Canada and the United States.

Country	Toll-free number
Anguilla	1-800-622-6232
Antigua	1-800-622-6232
Australia	011-800-622-6232-1
Austria	00-800-622-6232-1
Bahamas	1-800-389-0162
Bahrain	800-748
Barbardos	1-800-622-6232
Belgium	00-800-622-6232-1
Bermuda	1-800-622-6232
Brazil	00815-8622-6232
Cayman Islands	1-800-622-6232
Chile	1-800-201687
China	10800-1400151
Colombia	980-9-19-6232
Costa Rica	0800-015-0118
Denmark	00-800-622-6232-1
Dominica	1-800-622-6232
Dominican Republic	1-888-156-3126

Fiji	00800-7099
Finland (Telecom)	990-800-622-6232-1
Finland (Finnet)	00-800-622-6232-1
France	00-800-622-6232-1
Germany	00-800-622-6232-1
Greece	00800-10-800-622-6232
Grenada	1-800-622-6232
Hong Kong (HKTI)	001-800-622-6232-1
Hungary	00-800-13740
Iceland	800-8471
Indonesia	008-800-105-187
Ireland	00-800-622-6232-1
Israel	014-800-622-6232-1
Italy	800-873033
Jamaica	1-800-622-6232
Japan (IDC)	0061-800-622-6232-1
Japan (ITJ)	0041-800-622-6232-1
Japan (KDD)	001-800-622-6232-1
Korea (Dacom)	002-800-622-6232-1
Korea (Korea Telecom)	001-800-622-6232-1
Luxembourg	0800-3711
Macau	0800-375
Malaysia (Telecom Malaysia)	00-800-622-6232-1
Mexico	001-800-514-6232
Monserrat	1-800-622-6232
Netherlands	00-800-622-6232-1
New Zealand (Telecom New Zealand)	00-800-622-6232-1
Norway	00-800-622-6232-1
Philippines	1-800-1-110-0240
Poland	0-0-800-111-4325
Portugal	800-819-492
Puerto Rico	1-877-624-6232
Saudi Arabia	800-814-6232
Singapore (Singapore Telecom)	001-800-622-6232
South Africa	0800-992-792
Spain	900-98-1581
St. Kitts & Nevis	1-800-622-6232
St. Vincent & Grenadines	1-800-622-6232
Sweden (Tele2)	007-800-622-6232-1

Sweden (Telia)	009-800-622-6232-1
Switzerland	00-800-622-6232-1
Taiwan	00-800-622-6232-1
Thailand	001-800-15-8622-6232
Trinidad & Tobago	1-800-622-6232
Turks & Caicos	1-800-555-0060
UK (British Telecom & Mercury)	00-800-622-6232-1
Venezuela	800-1-5167
Virgin Islands (British)	1-800-622-6232
Virgin Islands (US)	1-877-621-6232

Please visit the Canada Site *www.canada.gc.ca/directories/ infor_e.html* for the most up-to-date international numbers for access to 1 800 O-Canada toll-free service.

7

The Priority System and Interview

THE PRIORITY SYSTEM

Your application will be dealt with according to the following priority system used by all Canadian immigration offices abroad:

1. Sponsored applications for husbands, wives, children under 19 and orphans.

2. Applicants who have a job offer validated in Canada by a Canada Employment Centre.

3. Entrepreneurs, Investors and Self-Employed persons.

4. Sponsored applications for parents and grandparents and all other sponsored applications not listed under priority 1 above.

5. Independent applications for employment, and all others.

The priority system is applied at each individual Canadian immigration office. For example, if you are in priority 5 with the Canadian High Commission in London, England, your application might take only a few months to process. However, if you are in that same priority with the Canadian Embassy in Manila in the Philippines your application may take much longer to process.

To complicate matters, the government is now assigning annual quotas to all offices abroad, so it is difficult to know if the prescribed priority system really has much meaning.

Please note that you can apply to any Canadian immigration office, even if you do not live in that area of the world. You must, however, be able to provide a mailing address within the processing area of the office to which you apply. The exception is individuals legally but temporarily residing in Canada as a visitor, student or under an employment authorisation who can use their Canadian address if applying through a Canadian immigration office in the United States. Normally, you are best advised to apply to the office in your own area, as that office has a better appreciation of local customs, and will probably be better able to fairly assess your qualifications.

However, many months of processing time can sometimes be saved by applying at a less busy office in the world, provided you are prepared to meet the expenses involved in travelling else-where for interview and medical examination.

After your application has been reviewed and provisionally approved, you should be called for an interview. The Canadian immigration office to which you sent your application will send you a letter indicating where and when you should present your-self for an interview, or, more probably, you will receive a letter stating you will be contacted at a later date.

The 'call-in-letter' when received will state all the additional documentation required.

PREPARING FOR THE INTERVIEW

You will meet a Canadian immigration officer for an interview, which may last from 30 minutes to 2 hours. It all depends on your situation. The officer will ask you a series of questions after they have examined your application. *Go prepared.*

Typical questions asked

There is no standard list of questions Canadian immigration officers use. Each officer may ask any question they wish to ask, so long as it pertains to your application. However, there are certain questions most officers ask prospective immigrants.

Accompanying persons

The officer will ask your name and who the people are accom-panying you, if there are any. Your family accompanying you to the interview might also be asked questions. The officer will then normally ask for verification of all the information you gave in the application form starting with your passport.

Documents

They will want to see your birth certificate to verify your place and date of birth. The officer will want your marriage or divorce papers to verify your marital status. You will have to produce your identity card, if you have one.

The officer will want to see proof of all your assets, such as bank statements and other documents. If you have a job offer in Canada, they will want to see some proof of that, such as a letter offering employment. They will want to see all your diplomas, degrees and certificates. The officer will also want to see proof of your work history and past earnings.

You will then be asked to sign the last page of the Application for Permanent Residence in front of the officer.

General questions
Then the officer will begin the questioning. Probably the most frequently asked question is 'Why do you want to immigrate to Canada?' You should, as in all your answers, be truthful and detailed.

You are not advised to answer by saying simply 'because I want to join my brother'. Indeed, you should tell the officer this if this is your motivation. But do not stop there. If, for example, you have visited Canada and liked Canada, tell the officer that. Tell the officer what you know about Canada, about its culture, way of life, and so on. If you believe Canada would be a good place to live and work, say so.

You can also answer the question by pointing out the lack of opportunities in your home country, if it is appropriate. If your home country is undergoing particular economic or political instability, you can point this out to the officer.

The officer will probably ask you about employment opportunities for you in Canada. They will want to know where in Canada you intend to go, how you will look for a job, and so on. You should have some knowledge of employment opportunities in your occupation in Canada to respond to these questions.

If you know there are good opportunities for you in Canada, tell the officer so. And tell them how you found out. Suggested methods to find out include going to your local library and reading a Canadian newspaper, which should also be available at all Canadian Embassies, High Commissions and Consulates. Or contact a relative or friend in Canada and ask him or her to find out about job opportunities for you.

The officer will want to know about your financial resources. How much money do you have to transfer to Canada? How much will you have with you when you arrive? You will have to show the officer that you have enough money immediately on hand to live on until you find a job or set up in business.

The officer might want to know what you know about Canada. For example, what is the weather like in the place you intend to reside? How much does a two bedroom apartment or flat cost there? Do you have some knowledge about life in Canada? Again, you might ask a friend or relative in Canada to find out this information for you.

The above questions are meant only as guidelines for you to prepare for the interview. Your interview with a Canadian immigration officer is the most important stage in the process with regard to the number of points you will receive on the Personal Suitability factor.

OUTCOME OF THE INTERVIEW

Your application may be provisionally approved on the basis of your coming to Canada for employment or as an entrepreneur, investor or self-employed person. You will then be issued medical examination instructions. Or your application may be refused at this point. The immigration officer may not give you their decision at the interview, but they will write to you later sending medical examination papers or stating that your application has been rejected.

If you are refused, there is unfortunately no formal avenue of appealing against the decision, unless you have been 'sponsored' by a close relative in Canada. However, if you truly believe you meet the requirements, you do have the right to argue the decision or to hire a consultant to argue for you. Such representations are sometimes successful as immigration officers do make mistakes.

More likely, however, you are going to have to take steps to improve your chances with a new application. Take a look again at the suggestions in this regard in Chapter 3.

8

The Clearance Checks

YOUR SECURITY CHECK

Unless you have any of the convictions outlined previously, or you have engaged in terrorist or subversive activities, you should have no difficulty passing the security check.

YOUR MEDICAL CHECK

Once you receive a letter from a Canadian immigration office informing you that a medical examination is required, you may indulge in a little rejoicing! **This letter is an indication that your application for Permanent Residence has been provisionally approved, and that you are well on your way to becoming an immigrant to Canada.**

The letter will come attached to a set of medical instructions and medical examination forms for yourself and your dependants. You and the physician examining you should carefully follow the instructions.

You should take the letter to the examining physician. You will also have to take your passport and/or identity card for identification.

The examining physician
You may be able to complete the examination with any physician of your choice, including your own doctor. However, in certain countries the Canadian government has designated certain doctors to examine prospective immigrants. If this is the case, a list of designated doctors will be given to you or you may be directed to a specific doctor.

It is up to you to make an appointment with the examining physician. Normally, you should undergo the examination within 60 to 90 days of the date the Canadian immigration office writes to you. You will have to pay the costs of the medical examination and any further tests or treatment which may be required.

The examining physician will send the medical forms to the appropriate address provided on the medical examination forms. Canadian immigration doctors will examine the results and forward their recommendations to the immigration office you are dealing with.

Results

If you have failed the medical examination outright, there is no formal appeal. However, you should be able to ask why you failed the medical examination so that you may be treated and cured and re-examined for immigration purposes.

If you pass the medical examination, a letter will be sent to you, usually within four (4) months, including your immigrant visa. Then you can present your passport and immigration visa at the port of entry. (Please note that Diplomatic Passports are not valid for immigration to Canada: you must have a regular passport.)

The results of the medical examination are valid for one year from the date of examination. You must proceed to Canada as an immigrant within this time period. **Canadian Immigrant Visas will not be extended for any reason**.

WHEN TO DEPART

You will have to immigrate to Canada within one year of your medical examination, even if it is a few months after the medical examination that you receive your visa. If you fail to immigrate within the validity of your visa, you must reapply and go through the whole process again, under whatever regulations are in effect at that time. In other words, if you fail to exercise your visa, there is no guarantee that a subsequent application will succeed.

9

What is an Immigrant Visa?

THE RECORD OF LANDING

Congratulations! The envelope you received to present to an immigration officer at the Canadian border or port of entry contains an immigrant visa called an **Immigrant Visa and Record of Landing**. There is no Canadian immigrant visa attached to or impressed in your passport, unlike the procedure in many other countries.

The Immigrant Visa and Record of Landing will contain the following information:

- your name
- date and place of birth
- country of citizenship
- accompanying family members
- passport particulars
- intended occupation.

The Visa will also contain two details of immediate importance to you. First, the expiration date. You *must* bring the Immigrant Visa and Record of Landing and enter Canada as an immigrant before that date. It will not be extended for any reason! Secondly, it will contain the terms and conditions attached to your status, if any. For example, the visa might state that you must establish a business within a specified period of time, usually within 2 years of your arrival. Whatever the terms and conditions set forth in the visa, you must fulfil them.

You may travel to Canada by any route you wish and enter through any Canadian port of entry.

THE PORT OF ENTRY CHECK

Immigration

You should give the immigration officer the envelope containing your visa. The officer will then complete certain formalities, such as asking you to sign it. The officer will then sign and attach a copy of the Record of Landing to your passport, and stamp your passport with a '**Permanent Resident**' stamp.

Customs

You will then have to proceed through Canadian Customs. You may enter Canada with all your household and personal goods without paying any duty provided they have been in your use prior to migrating. This includes such items as your furniture, automobiles, jewellery, and so on. Customs regulations are beyond the scope of this book, and you should check with the nearest Canadian High Commission, Embassy or Consulate if you have any questions before leaving your home country.

- **After you have cleared Canadian Customs, you will enter Canada as a permanent resident (landed immigrant).**

WHAT IS A LANDED IMMIGRANT OR PERMANENT RESIDENT?

A **Landed Immigrant** or **Permanent Resident** enjoys most of the rights of a Canadian citizen.

You may, as an immigrant, engage in any activity, work in any employment, and live wherever in Canada you would like to. You are under no obligation to register with the police or immigration as in many other countries. However, remember that there might be certain conditions attached to your immigrant visa that you must fulfil. Also, you will want to register yourself and your dependants in the government-sponsored medical care plan of the province in which you are going to live as soon as possible after arrival. You will also need to apply for a **Social Insurance Number** (SIN card) in order to take up employment in Canada.

Permanent residence confers on you all the legal rights of Canadian citizenship, with a few minor exceptions. You are guaranteed fundamental rights of all Canadians.

Restrictions

You may not vote, however, in any federal election or be eligible to run as a candidate in any election. You may not be able to engage in certain professions, such as practising law or medicine, unless you are a Canadian citizen, depending on the regulations of the province in which you reside. There are also certain restrictions on drawing old age pensions or general welfare payments. For the most part, however, you will be free to do anything you want.

APPLYING FOR CANADIAN CITIZENSHIP

After three years of residency in Canada as a permanent resident (or less if you resided in Canada previously as a non-immigrant, perhaps as a student or under an employment visa) you will be eligible to apply for Canadian citizenship.

HOW NOT TO LOSE YOUR IMMIGRANT STATUS

Before you arrive . . .

There are several ways you could lose your immigrant visa **before you arrive in Canada, but after your immigrant visa has been issued**. If you are convicted of serious offences, have engaged in or might engage in espionage or terrorism, you might be excluded from entering into Canada.

After you arrive . . .

You can lose your immigrant status even once you are in Canada. If you received your visa by means of false documents or misleading statements; if you wilfully fail to support yourself or your family; if you have broken some condition of your visa such as failing to establish a business you said you would; if you are convicted of a serious offence in Canada prior to becoming a citizen, you may be forced to leave.

Returning Resident Permits

You may also lose your immigrant status if you are outside Canada for over 183 days in any twelve month period, unless you have a **Returning Resident Permit**. You should note that you should not be out of Canada for more than 183 days in *any* twelve month period, not just the calendar year from January to December.

If you intend to be out of Canada for a prolonged period of time, you should apply for a Returning Resident Permit, before leaving. If you are outside Canada and find for some unforeseen reason that you have to remain outside Canada for over 183 days or you simply did not obtain a Returning Resident Permit before leaving Canada, you may apply for one at any Canadian immigration office outside Canada.

A Returning Resident Permit is usually valid for one year only, but it may be issued or extended for up to two years. You should return to Canada before the permit expires, in order to protect your immigrant status.

There are no standard reasons why a Returning Resident Permit may be issued. You might be going abroad to study, to work, or to go on a long trip. But if you are planning to set up your family in Canada, and then return to your former employment abroad, you will not be issued a Returning Resident Permit. Your principal place of residence has to be in Canada. There has to be some extraordinary reason why you have to be outside Canada for a prolonged period, such as being employed in Canada by an international Canadian firm which decides to transfer you to a position abroad. Of course, once you acquire Canadian citizenship, you may leave Canada for as long as you want. A Canadian citizen always has the right to enter Canada.

10

Conclusion

I have tried to explain Canadian immigration procedures and policy clearly and concisely. Perhaps you will now be able to proceed with your application without any further assistance from anyone except a Canadian immigration office.

You should, at this point, have gained a good overall understanding regarding immigrating to Canada and know the different application methods. You should also know which category to apply in, how to apply as a Sponsored Dependant or an Independent Applicant, how to determine your chances of succeeding, and how to fill in and document the application forms.

You should have some knowledge about what to do once you obtain your visa, and how not to lose your immigrant status once in Canada.

APPEALS

I have deliberately left out certain parts of the overall immigration process, such as those that relate to visitors and students to Canada and refugees, since this book is primarily designed to aid applicants for permanent residence who are outside Canada.

I have also left out the appeal process and procedure. It is not possible to rely on any guide such as this to appeal against a refused application. Instead, you should contact a competent immigration consultant to help you.

In short, this book covers the most usual situations and procedures. There are many exceptions made in immigration procedures, usually for humanitarian and compassionate reasons. In addition, procedures and policies may exist which have limited application but which could help you. This is where a competent and experienced immigration consultant can particularly help you.

FAMILY BUSINESSES

For example, one such exception concerns *Family Businesses and the Processing of Job Offers to Relatives*. Independent applicants who have a relative in Canada but who cannot meet the point system may nevertheless comply if coming forward to join an existing family oriented business in Canada, provided the relative already in Canada can, among other things, demonstrate a genuine need to employ a relative in the business, rather than someone already resident in Canada. (However, I have to tell you that this provision will probably be withdrawn under the forthcoming new regulations.)

If you have reason to believe your particular situation warrants special consideration or is unique in some way, then you should seek professional assistance.

OBTAINING PROFESSIONAL HELP

This brings me to the final point: that of third-party involvement in the Canadian immigration process. Unfortunately, there are persons within and outside Canada who offer incompetent, misleading and inaccurate advice to prospective immigrants for exorbitant fees.

By the very fact that you have read this book and have gained a knowledge of Canada's immigration procedures and policies, you should be able to judge the competency of any such adviser and be able to pinpoint any inaccurate counsel you receive.

You are strongly advised to ask yourself certain questions about any such adviser before proceeding. What, for example, are the adviser's credentials in Canadian immigration matters? What are the services the adviser offers? Do they make claims they cannot possibly fulfill, such as assurances or guarantees you will be granted an immigrant visa? What is their track record? How many years have they been in business? How many cases have they dealt with, and what percentage of their cases succeed? You should also ask a friend or relative in Canada to check them out for you.

That is not to say, however, that there are not reputable, experienced and competent Canadian immigration consultants who genuinely aid prospective immigrants. Indeed, there are many instances, such as business establishment cases, where the assistance of consultants is recommended, and appeals to the

Immigration Appeal Board or the Federal Court of Appeals where counsel is essential.

M. J. Bjarnason & Associates Ltd has assisted several thousand individuals and families to immigrate to Canada from all over the world who are now successfully settled from coast to coast. Should you require more specific assistance concerning your individual situation, please contact this service (for address please see the useful addresses section on page 175).

Useful Addresses

CANADIAN IMMIGRATION COUNSELLING

M. J. Bjarnason & Associates Co. Ltd., 187 Maxome Avenue, Toronto, Ontario, Canada M2M 3L1. Tel: (416) 766-2313. Fax: (416) 766-8263. Email: mjbjarn@attglobal.net. Internet: *http://mjbjarnason.com*

Organization of Professional Immigration Consultants (OPIC), 873 Broadview Avenue, Toronto, Ontario, Canada M4K 2P9. Tel: (416) 469-0750. Internet: *http://www.opic.org*

TRAVEL

All-Canada Travel & Holidays Ltd, Sunway House, Raglan Street, Lowestoft, Suffolk, NR32 2LW. Tel: (01502) 585825.

Canadian Airlines International Ltd, 23–59 Staines Road, Hounslow, Middlesex TW3 3HE. Tel: (020) 8577 7722.

Canadian Universities Travel Services (UK) Ltd, 295a Regent Street, London W1R 7YA. Tel: (020) 7255 2191.

Fairmont Hotels & Resorts, 62–65 Trafalgar Square, London WC2N 5DY. Tel: (020) 7389 1126. Internet: *http://www.fairmont.com.*

FINANCIAL SERVICES

Canadian Imperial Bank of Commerce, Cottons Centre, Cotton Lane, London SE1 2QL. Tel: (020) 7234 6000.

Toronto-Dominion Bank, Triton Court, Finsbury Square, London EC2A 1DB. Tel: (020) 7920 0272.

OTHER

British Columbia House, 1 Regent Street, London SW1Y 4NS. Tel: (020) 7930 6857.

Canadian Broadcasting Corporation, 43 Great Titchfield Street, London W1W 7DA. Tel: (020) 7412 9200.

Quebec House, 59 Pall Mall, London SW1Y 5JH. Tel: (020) 7766 5900.

OTHER USEFUL ORGANISATIONS

Accounting

Canadian Association of Certified Executive Accountants, No. 240, 2415 Holly Lane, Ottawa, Ontario K1V 7PZ. Tel: (613) 521 0620.

Canadian Institute of Chartered Accountants, 277 Wellington Street West, Toronto, Ontario M5V 3H2. Tel: (416) 977 3222.

Society of Management Accountants of Canada, 1 Robert Speck Parkway, Suite 1400, Mississuaga, Ontario L42 3M3. Tel: (905) 949 3106. E-mail: info@cma-canada.org

Agriculture and farming

Canadian Federation of Agriculture, No. 1101, 75 Albert Street, Ottawa, Ontario K1P 5E7. Tel: (613) 236 3633.

National Farmers Union, 2717 Wentz Avenue, Saksatoon, Saskatchewan S7K 4B6. Tel: (306) 652 9465. Fax: (306) 664 6226. Internet: *http://www.nfu.ca*

Animals

Canadian Veterinary Medical Association, 339 Booth Street, Ottawa, Ontario K1R 7K1. Tel: (613) 236 1162.

Canadian Wildlife Federation, 350 Michael Cowpland Drive, Kanata, Ontario. Tel: (613) 599 9594.

Architecture

Royal Architectural Institute of Canada, No. 330, 55 Murray Street, Ottawa, Ontario K1N 5M3. Tel: (613) 241 3600.

Automotive

Canadian Automobile Association, 1145 Hunt Club, Ottawa, Ontario K1V 0Y3. Tel: (613) 247 0117.

Broadcasting

Canadian Association of Broadcasters, 306–350 Sparks, Ottawa, Ontario K1R 7S8. Tel: (613) 233 4035.

Building and construction
Canadian Construction Association, 75 Albert Street, Ottawa, Ontario K1P 5E7. Tel: (613) 236 9455.

Business
Better Business Bureau of Metropolitan Toronto Inc., No. 403, 1st St John's Road, Toronto, Ontario M6P 4C7. Tel: (416) 766 5744.

Canadian Association of Family Enterprise, 1163 Sylvester, Lefroy, Ontario. Tel: (705) 456 4900.

Canadian Institute of Marketing, 41 Capital Drive, Nepean, Ontario K2G 0E7. Tel: (613) 727 0954.

Canadian Organization of Small Business Inc, 10010 107A Avenue Nw, Edmonton, Alberta T5H 4H8. Tel: (403) 423 2672.

Canadian Professional Sales Association, No. 310, 145 Wellington Street West, Toronto, Ontario M5J 1H8. Tel: (416) 408 2685.

Chemical industry
The Chemical Institute of Canada, No. 550, 130 Slater Street, Ottawa, Ontario K1P 6E2. Tel: (613) 232 6252.

Children & youth
Boys & Girls Clubs of Canada, No. 703, 7030 Woodbine Avenue, Markham, Ontario L3R 6G2. Tel: (416) 477 7272.

Girl Guides of Canada, 50 Merton Street, Toronto, Ontario M4S 1A3. Tel: (416) 487 5281.

Citizenship & immigration
Canadian Citizenship Federation, No. 402, 396 Cooper Street, Ottawa Ontario K2P 2H7. Tel: (613) 235 1467.

Canadian Immigration Historical Society, PO Box 9502, Ottawa, Ontario K1G 3V2. Tel: (888) 242 2100.

Citizenship Council of Manitoba Inc., 406 Edmonton Street, Winnipeg, Manitoba R3B 2M2. Tel: (204) 943 9158.

Jewish Immigrant Aid Services of Canada, No. 325, 4600 Bathurst Street, Toronto, Ontario M2R 3V3. Tel: (416) 630 9501.

National Organization of Immigrants & Visible Minority Women of Canada, 225–219 Argyle Avenue, Ottawa, Ontario. Tel: (613) 232 0689.

Ontario Council of Agencies Serving Immigrants, 110 Eglington Avenue West, Toronto, Ontario M6C 14R. Tel: (416) 322 4950.

Organization of Professional Immigration Consultants, 873 Broadview Avenue, Toronto, Ontario M4K 2P9. Tel: (416) 499 0750.

Consumers

Consumers' Association of Canada, 267 O'Connor, Ottawa,, Ontario. Tel: (613) 238 2533.

Cultural

Association of Canadian Clubs, 237 Nepean Street, Ottawa, Ontario K2P 0B7. Tel: (613) 236 8288.

English-Speaking Union of Canada, 30 Elm Avenue, Toronto, Ontario. Tel: (416) 925 6623.

The Royal Commonwealth Society, Commonwealth House, 18 Northumberland Avenue, London WC2N 5BJ, United Kingdom. Tel: (020) 7930 6733.

Society for Educational Visits & Exchanges in Canada, 57 Auriga Drive, Nepean, Ontario K2E 8B2. Tel: (613) 998 3760.

Disability

Canadian Disability Rights Council, No. 400–500, Portage Avenue, Winnipeg, Manitoba. Tel: (204) 774 7158.

Economics

Canadian Economics Association, University of Toronto, Ontario, M5S 3G7. Tel: (416) 978 6295.

Education

Association of Universities & Colleges of Canada, 320–350 Albert Street, Ottawa, Ontario K1P 5N1. Tel: (613) 563 1236.

Canadian Federation of Students, No. 600, 170 Metcalfe Street, Ottawa, Ontario K2P 1P3. Tel: (613) 232 7394.

Canadian Home & School & Parent-Teacher Federation, 250 Holland Avenue, Ottawa, Ontario K1Y 0Y6. Tel: (613) 798 2837.

Canadian Teachers' Federation, 110 Argyle Street, Ottawa, Ontario K2P 1B4. Tel: (613) 232 1505.

Energy
Canadian Institute of Energy, No. 1600, 734–7 Avenue South West, Calgary, Alberta T2P 3P8. Tel: (403) 262 6969. Fax: (403) 269 2787.

Engineering
Canadian Council of Professional Engineers, No. 401, 116 Albert Street, Ottawa, Ontario K1P 5G3. Tel: (613) 232 2474.

Events
Canadian Film Institute, 2 Daly, Ottawa, Ontario K1N 6E2. Tel: (613) 232 6727.

Canadian Film & Television Production Association, 830–20 Totonto Street, Totonto, Ontario M5C 2B8. Tel: (416) 304 0277.

Federation of Canadian Music Festivals, 1034 Chestnut Avenue, Moose Jaw, Saskatchewan S6H 1A6. Tel: (306) 693 7087.

Finance
Association of Canadian Venture Capital Companies, No. 1000, 120 Eglington Avenue East, Toronto, Ontario M4P 1EZ.

Canadian Association of Investment Clubs, 49 The Donway, PO Box 174, Toronto, Ontario M5J 1E6. Tel: (416) 488 2242.

Canadian Bankers' Association, 199 Bay Street, Toronto, Ontario M5X 1E1. Tel: (416) 362 6092.

Health & medical
Canadian Dental Association, 1815 Alta Vista Drive, Ottawa, Ontario K1G 3Y6. Tel: (613) 523 1770.

Canadian Medical Association, 1867 Alta Vista Drive, PO Box 8050, Ottawa, Ontario K1G 3Y6. Tel: (613) 731 9331.

Canadian Nurses Association, 50 The Driveway, Ottawa, Ontario K2P 1E2. Tel: (613) 237 2133.

Information management
Information Technology Association of Canada, 2800 Skymark Avenue, Cooksville, Ontario L4W 5A6. Tel: (905) 602 8345.

Insurance industry
Insurance Bureau of Canada, No. 180, 151 Yonge Street, Toronto, Ontario M5C 2W7. Tel: (416) 362 2031.

International cooperation

Canadian Council for International Cooperation, No. 300, One Nicholas Street, Ottawa, Ontario K1N 7B7. Tel: (613) 241 7007.

Friends of the Earth, 260 St Patrick, Ottawa, Ontario. Tel: (613) 241 0085.

Management & administration

Institute of Chartered Secretaries & Administrators, No. 225, 55 St Clair Avenue West, Toronto, Ontario M4V 297. Tel: (416) 944 9727.

Professional Secretaries International, 10502 North West Ambassador Drive, PO Box 20404, Kansas City, Missouri MO 64195-0404 USA. Tel: (816) 891 6600. Fax: (816) 891 9118

Real estate

The Canadian Real Estate Association, No. 1600, 344 Slater Street, Canada Building, Ottawa, Ontario K1R 7Y3. Tel: (613) 237 7111. Fax: (613) 234 2567.

Restaurants, bars, food services

Canadian Restaurant & Foodservices Association, No. 1201, 80 Bloor Street West, Toronto, Ontario M5S 2V1. Tel: (416) 923 8416.

Senior citizens

Canadian Association of Retired Persons, No. 1304, 27 Queen Street East, Toronto, Ontario M5C 2M6. Tel: (416) 363 8748.

Taxation

Canadian Federation of Tax Consultants, No. 502, 161 Eglinton Avenue East, Toronto, Ontario M4P 1J5. Tel: (416) 488 5404.

Tourism & travel

Tourism Industry Association of Canada, No. 1016, 130 Albert Street, Ottawa, Ontario K1P 5G4. Tel: (613) 238 3853.

Useful Government of Canada web sites

The Government of Canada main web site (*www.canada.gc.ca*) provides a wealth of information for prospective immigrants. Here are some of the sites you will find of interest:

Citizenship and Immigration Canada Welcomes Foreign Students and **Studying in Canada: A Guide for Foreign Students** available online under 'visitors' and then 'studying in Canada' at *www.cic.gc.ca.*

The **National Job Bank** (*www.jb.ge.hrdc.drhc.gc.ca*) is a comprehensive online database of thousands of jobs, and work or business opportunities across Canada.

The **Electronic Labour Exchange** (*www.ele.hrdc.drhc.gc.ca*) is an Internet job-searching service that connects you with potential employers at the click of a button.

Canada WorkInfoNet (*www.workinfonet.ca*) is a unique web site that can help you plan and carry out your job search. It covers everything from CV writing to interview techniques, and from potential employment opportunities to starting your own business.

SkillNet.ca is a network of job and career infomation web sites.

The **National Atlas of Canada Online** (*www.atlas.gc.ca*) provides maps and information about Canada's geography.

How to Become a Canadian Citizen explains the requirements of citizenship and the application process for permanent residence: go to the 'publications' section and scroll down to 'citizenship' at *www.cic.gc.ca.*

Family sponsorship allows citizens and permanent residents to sponsor immediate family members for immigration to Canada. Find out more online under 'immigrants' and then 'immigrating to Canada' at *www.cic.ca.*

Welcome to Canada: What You Should Know is a comprehensive guide for newcomers to Canada. It includes sections on health services, finding a job, language training, education, Canadian law, etc. View online at *www.cic.gc.ca* by going to 'publications' then scrolling down to 'living in Canada'.

Citizenship is the next step after becoming an immigrant. People interested in applying as immigrants can consult *www.cic.gc.ca* under 'publications' and then 'immigrating to Canada'.

Language Instruction for Newcomers to Canada (LINC) provides basic language instruction for adult immigrants. View this material online at *www.cic.gc.ca* by going to 'publications', then clicking on 'living in Canada'.

Coming Back to Canada: Returning Residents Permits explains what to do if you are a permanent resident of Canada but not a Canadian Citizen, and plan to stay outside Canada for an extended period. This document is available online under 'immigrants' and then 'living in Canada' at *www.cic.gc.ca.*

Bon Voyage, But . . . provides a list of the addresses and telephone numbers of Canadian Consulates, Embassies and High Commissions around the world. It is available at *www.dfaitmaeci.gc.ca* by clicking on 'travel' then on 'publications'.

Information On Settling In Canada: Personal Effects – guidance on taking personal effects to Canada, you can find the customs related information at *www.rc.ge.ca.*

Information on Occupations or Professions that may require licensing in Canada are found at *www.workdestinations.org* (Note: select a destination, then go to 'regulated occupations'.)

Further Reading

Canada News, Outbound Newspapers, 1 Commercial Road, Eastbourne, East Sussex BN21 3XQ. Tel: (01323) 412001. News and features for visitors and migrants to Canada.

Can-UK Link, magazine of the Canada-UK Chamber of Commerce, British Columbia House, 3 Regent Street, London SW1Y 4NZ. Tel: (020) 7930 7711. Fax: (020) 7930 9703.

Canadabooks International, The Warehouse, Old Mead Road, Elsenham, Bishops Stortford, Hertfordshire. Tel: (01279) 814228.

Directory of Associations in Canada, Micromedia Ltd, 20 Victoria Street, Toronto M5C 2N8. Comprehensive reference source which costs in excess of Can.$200.

Directory of Canadian Companies Overseas, Overseas Employment Services, PO Box 460, Town of Mount Royal, Quebec H3P 3C7.

Directory of Canadian Employment Agencies, Overseas Consultants, PO Box 152, Douglas, Isle of Man.

Directory of Canadian Firms Overseas, Overseas Consultants, PO Box 152, Douglas, Isle of Man.

Toronto Globe & Mail, 444 Front Street West, Toronto, Ontario. Leading national newspaper.

Toronto Star Newspapers, UK office, 60 Great Titchfield Street, London W1P 7AE. Tel: (020) 7637 7187.

Working Abroad, Jonathan Golding, International Venture Handbooks, Plymbridge House, Estover Road, Plymouth PL6 7PZ. Tel: (01752) 202301. Essential financial advice for prospective British expatriates and their employers, covering tax, offshore investment, contract negotiation and similar matters.

Index

LIVING AND WORKING IN CANADA
A new life in Canada – all you need to know

Benjamin A Kranc & Karina Roman

Canada is a vast, beautiful country with many opportunities. This inspiring book helps you assess if it's the place for you and, if so, guides you through the whole Canadian immigration process. There's information on finding a place to live, getting a job, starting a business and education too – everything from pre-school to university life. Everyday issues such as rules of the road, shopping, and simply having fun are covered, together with a list of useful contacts and addresses. Benjamin A. Kranc is a Specialist Lawyer in Immigration Law, Karina Roman is a journalist who has freelanced for the *National Post*, amongst other publications.

144pp. illus. 1 85703 553 4.

TEACHING ABROAD
How and where to find teaching and lecturing jobs worldwide

Roger Jones

This revised and updated third edition meets a real demand for practical and realistic information. 'Comprehensive and well researched – invaluable.' *Education*. 'Covers all the main aspects of the subject'. *Wonderlust*. 'A wonderful book . . . reviews teaching opportunities in over 180 countries, and includes addresses for the Ministry of Education in each.' *Career Bookstore (Canada Employment Weekly)*.

192pp. illus. 1 85703 276 4. 3rd edition.

SPENDING A YEAR ABROAD
A guide to opportunities for self-development and discovery around the world
Nick Vandome

A year abroad is for anyone – whether you're a student, grandparent or considering a mid-life break. If you want to do it you can, and this book explores the wealth of options open to you. It's packed full of vital information – including 228 useful organisations and contact addresses. It looks at where to go, ways to travel, explores work opportunities and even includes experiences from people who have been there and done it. 'Excellent.' *Careers Guidance Today.* 'Required reading.' *School Librarian Journal.*

176pp. illus. 1 85703 544 5. 4th edition.

FINDING VOLUNTARY WORK ABROAD
All the information you need for getting valuable work experience overseas
Mark Hempshell

The updated third edition of this practical handbook helps you check out the skills, qualifications and experience you might need for all kinds of voluntary work, and find out about the variety of opportunities throughout the world.

160pp. illus. 1 85703 496 1. 3rd edition.

GETTING A JOB IN CANADA
Secure a well-paid job and a great new life style
Valerie Gerrard

Fully updated for its second edition, this reliable guide takes you through the whole process of achieving permission to work, finding and landing the right job and settling in. Valerie Gerrard is a Canadian with many year's experience of working in Canada, and personal experience of helping others to relocate there. '. . . well organised and interesting . . . aimed at anyone considering moving to Canada; from students looking for vacation work to people new to the job scene through to job changers' *University of Salford Careers Advisory Service.*

176pp. illus. 1 85703 465 1. 2nd edition.

GETTING INTO AMERICA
The immigration guide to finding a new life in the USA
Henry G. Liebman

'An invaluable resource offering practical and comprehensive answers without having to consult an expensive immigration lawyer. Recommended.' *Overseas Jobs Express.* Written by an experienced immigration lawyer, this thorough and accessible handbook guides you through the whole immigration process, and shows how to obtain the best visa for your requirements – whether for work, investment, study or permanent residence.

144pp. illus. 1 85703 490 2.

GETTING A JOB ABROAD
The handbook for the international jobseeker: where the jobs are, how to get them

Roger Jones

Now in its fifth edition, this is the handbook for anyone planning to spend a period of work abroad. '. . . highly informative . . . lots of hard information and a first class reference section.' *The Escape Committee Newsletter.* 'An excellent addition to any careers library . . . compact and realistic . . . There is a wide range of reference addresses covering employment agencies, specialist newspapers, a comprehensive booklist and helpful addresses . . . All readers, whether careers officers, young adults or more mature adults will find a use for this book.' *Newscheck, COIC.*

336pp. illus. 1 85703 418 X. 5th edition.

GETTING A JOB IN AMERICA
How to find the right employment opportunities and contacts

Roger Jones

This handbook is invaluable for everyone planning to work in the US, whether on a short-term vacation assignment, secondment or contract, or on a permanent basis. Based on the experience of individuals, companies and recruitment agencies, the book covers the range of jobs available, locations, pay and conditions, and how to get hired. 'Essential for anyone who is thinking of working in the US.' *Going USA.* 'For young people considering a US exchange or summer employment, the section on vacation jobs is particularly worthwhile.' *Newscheck, Careers Service Bulletin.*

224pp illus. 1 85703 372 8. 5th edition.